Mometrix

TEST PREPARATION

Common Core Grade 11 English Language Arts Secrets Study Guide

DEAR FUTURE EXAM SUCCESS STORY

First of all, **THANK YOU** for purchasing Mometrix study materials!

Second, congratulations! You are one of the few determined test-takers who are committed to doing whatever it takes to excel on your exam. **You have come to the right place.** We developed these study materials with one goal in mind: to deliver you the information you need in a format that's concise and easy to use.

In addition to optimizing your guide for the content of the test, we've outlined our recommended steps for breaking down the preparation process into small, attainable goals so you can make sure you stay on track.

We've also analyzed the entire test-taking process, identifying the most common pitfalls and showing how you can overcome them and be ready for any curveball the test throws you.

Standardized testing is one of the biggest obstacles on your road to success, which only increases the importance of doing well in the high-pressure, high-stakes environment of test day. Your results on this test could have a significant impact on your future, and this guide provides the information and practical advice to help you achieve your full potential on test day.

Your success is our success

We would love to hear from you! If you would like to share the story of your exam success or if you have any questions or comments in regard to our products, please contact us at **800-673-8175** or **support@mometrix.com**.

Thanks again for your business and we wish you continued success!

Sincerely,
The Mometrix Test Preparation Team

Need more help? Check out our flashcards at:
http://MometrixFlashcards.com/CCSS

Written and edited by the Mometrix Exam Secrets Test Prep Team
Printed in the United States of America

TABLE OF CONTENTS

Introduction

Thank you for purchasing this resource! You have made the choice to prepare yourself for a test that could have a huge impact on your future, and this guide is designed to help you be fully ready for test day. Obviously, it's important to have a solid understanding of the test material, but you also need to be prepared for the unique environment and stressors of the test, so that you can perform to the best of your abilities.

For this purpose, the first section that appears in this guide is the **Secret Keys**. We've devoted countless hours to meticulously researching what works and what doesn't, and we've boiled down our findings to the five most impactful steps you can take to improve your performance on the test. We start at the beginning with study planning and move through the preparation process, all the way to the testing strategies that will help you get the most out of what you know when you're finally sitting in front of the test.

We recommend that you start preparing for your test as far in advance as possible. However, if you've bought this guide as a last-minute study resource and only have a few days before your test, we recommend that you skip over the first two Secret Keys since they address a long-term study plan.

If you struggle with **test anxiety**, we strongly encourage you to check out our recommendations for how you can overcome it. Test anxiety is a formidable foe, but it can be beaten, and we want to make sure you have the tools you need to defeat it.

Secret Key #1 – Plan Big, Study Small

There's a lot riding on your performance. If you want to ace this test, you're going to need to keep your skills sharp and the material fresh in your mind. You need a plan that lets you review everything you need to know while still fitting in your schedule. We'll break this strategy down into three categories.

Information Organization

Start with the information you already have: the official test outline. From this, you can make a complete list of all the concepts you need to cover before the test. Organize these concepts into groups that can be studied together, and create a list of any related vocabulary you need to learn so you can brush up on any difficult terms. You'll want to keep this vocabulary list handy once you actually start studying since you may need to add to it along the way.

Time Management

Once you have your set of study concepts, decide how to spread them out over the time you have left before the test. Break your study plan into small, clear goals so you have a manageable task for each day and know exactly what you're doing. Then just focus on one small step at a time. When you manage your time this way, you don't need to spend hours at a time studying. Studying a small block of content for a short period each day helps you retain information better and avoid stressing over how much you have left to do. You can relax knowing that you have a plan to cover everything in time. In order for this strategy to be effective though, you have to start studying early and stick to your schedule. Avoid the exhaustion and futility that comes from last-minute cramming!

Study Environment

The environment you study in has a big impact on your learning. Studying in a coffee shop, while probably more enjoyable, is not likely to be as fruitful as studying in a quiet room. It's important to keep distractions to a minimum. You're only planning to study for a short block of time, so make the most of it. Don't pause to check your phone or get up to find a snack. It's also important to **avoid multitasking**. Research has consistently shown that multitasking will make your studying dramatically less effective. Your study area should also be comfortable and well-lit so you don't have the distraction of straining your eyes or sitting on an uncomfortable chair.

The time of day you study is also important. You want to be rested and alert. Don't wait until just before bedtime. Study when you'll be most likely to comprehend and remember. Even better, if you know what time of day your test will be, set that time aside for study. That way your brain will be used to working on that subject at that specific time and you'll have a better chance of recalling information.

Finally, it can be helpful to team up with others who are studying for the same test. Your actual studying should be done in as isolated an environment as possible, but the work of organizing the information and setting up the study plan can be divided up. In between study sessions, you can discuss with your teammates the concepts that you're all studying and quiz each other on the details. Just be sure that your teammates are as serious about the test as you are. If you find that your study time is being replaced with social time, you might need to find a new team.

Secret Key #2 – Make Your Studying Count

You're devoting a lot of time and effort to preparing for this test, so you want to be absolutely certain it will pay off. This means doing more than just reading the content and hoping you can remember it on test day. It's important to make every minute of study count. There are two main areas you can focus on to make your studying count.

Retention

It doesn't matter how much time you study if you can't remember the material. You need to make sure you are retaining the concepts. To check your retention of the information you're learning, try recalling it at later times with minimal prompting. Try carrying around flashcards and glance at one or two from time to time or ask a friend who's also studying for the test to quiz you.

To enhance your retention, look for ways to put the information into practice so that you can apply it rather than simply recalling it. If you're using the information in practical ways, it will be much easier to remember. Similarly, it helps to solidify a concept in your mind if you're not only reading it to yourself but also explaining it to someone else. Ask a friend to let you teach them about a concept you're a little shaky on (or speak aloud to an imaginary audience if necessary). As you try to summarize, define, give examples, and answer your friend's questions, you'll understand the concepts better and they will stay with you longer. Finally, step back for a big picture view and ask yourself how each piece of information fits with the whole subject. When you link the different concepts together and see them working together as a whole, it's easier to remember the individual components.

Finally, practice showing your work on any multi-step problems, even if you're just studying. Writing out each step you take to solve a problem will help solidify the process in your mind, and you'll be more likely to remember it during the test.

Modality

Modality simply refers to the means or method by which you study. Choosing a study modality that fits your own individual learning style is crucial. No two people learn best in exactly the same way, so it's important to know your strengths and use them to your advantage.

For example, if you learn best by visualization, focus on visualizing a concept in your mind and draw an image or a diagram. Try color-coding your notes, illustrating them, or creating symbols that will trigger your mind to recall a learned concept. If you learn best by hearing or discussing information, find a study partner who learns the same way or read aloud to yourself. Think about how to put the information in your own words. Imagine that you are giving a lecture on the topic and record yourself so you can listen to it later.

For any learning style, flashcards can be helpful. Organize the information so you can take advantage of spare moments to review. Underline key words or phrases. Use different colors for different categories. Mnemonic devices (such as creating a short list in which every item starts with the same letter) can also help with retention. Find what works best for you and use it to store the information in your mind most effectively and easily.

Secret Key #3 – Practice the Right Way

Your success on test day depends not only on how many hours you put into preparing, but also on whether you prepared the right way. It's good to check along the way to see if your studying is paying off. One of the most effective ways to do this is by taking practice tests to evaluate your progress. Practice tests are useful because they show exactly where you need to improve. Every time you take a practice test, pay special attention to these three groups of questions:

- The questions you got wrong
- The questions you had to guess on, even if you guessed right
- The questions you found difficult or slow to work through

This will show you exactly what your weak areas are, and where you need to devote more study time. Ask yourself why each of these questions gave you trouble. Was it because you didn't understand the material? Was it because you didn't remember the vocabulary? Do you need more repetitions on this type of question to build speed and confidence? Dig into those questions and figure out how you can strengthen your weak areas as you go back to review the material.

Additionally, many practice tests have a section explaining the answer choices. It can be tempting to read the explanation and think that you now have a good understanding of the concept. However, an explanation likely only covers part of the question's broader context. Even if the explanation makes perfect sense, **go back and investigate** every concept related to the question until you're positive you have a thorough understanding.

As you go along, keep in mind that the practice test is just that: practice. Memorizing these questions and answers will not be very helpful on the actual test because it is unlikely to have any of the same exact questions. If you only know the right answers to the sample questions, you won't be prepared for the real thing. **Study the concepts** until you understand them fully, and then you'll be able to answer any question that shows up on the test.

It's important to wait on the practice tests until you're ready. If you take a test on your first day of study, you may be overwhelmed by the amount of material covered and how much you need to learn. Work up to it gradually.

On test day, you'll need to be prepared for answering questions, managing your time, and using the test-taking strategies you've learned. It's a lot to balance, like a mental marathon that will have a big impact on your future. Like training for a marathon, you'll need to start slowly and work your way up. When test day arrives, you'll be ready.

Start with the strategies you've read in the first two Secret Keys—plan your course and study in the way that works best for you. If you have time, consider using multiple study resources to get different approaches to the same concepts. It can be helpful to see difficult concepts from more than one angle. Then find a good source for practice tests. Many times, the test website will suggest potential study resources or provide sample tests.

Practice Test Strategy

If you're able to find at least three practice tests, we recommend this strategy:

Untimed and Open-Book Practice

Take the first test with no time constraints and with your notes and study guide handy. Take your time and focus on applying the strategies you've learned.

Timed and Open-Book Practice

Take the second practice test open-book as well, but set a timer and practice pacing yourself to finish in time.

Timed and Closed-Book Practice

Take any other practice tests as if it were test day. Set a timer and put away your study materials. Sit at a table or desk in a quiet room, imagine yourself at the testing center, and answer questions as quickly and accurately as possible.

Keep repeating timed and closed-book tests on a regular basis until you run out of practice tests or it's time for the actual test. Your mind will be ready for the schedule and stress of test day, and you'll be able to focus on recalling the material you've learned.

Secret Key #4 – Pace Yourself

Once you're fully prepared for the material on the test, your biggest challenge on test day will be managing your time. Just knowing that the clock is ticking can make you panic even if you have plenty of time left. Work on pacing yourself so you can build confidence against the time constraints of the exam. Pacing is a difficult skill to master, especially in a high-pressure environment, so **practice is vital**.

Set time expectations for your pace based on how much time is available. For example, if a section has 60 questions and the time limit is 30 minutes, you know you have to average 30 seconds or less per question in order to answer them all. Although 30 seconds is the hard limit, set 25 seconds per question as your goal, so you reserve extra time to spend on harder questions. When you budget extra time for the harder questions, you no longer have any reason to stress when those questions take longer to answer.

Don't let this time expectation distract you from working through the test at a calm, steady pace, but keep it in mind so you don't spend too much time on any one question. Recognize that taking extra time on one question you don't understand may keep you from answering two that you do understand later in the test. If your time limit for a question is up and you're still not sure of the answer, mark it and move on, and come back to it later if the time and the test format allow. If the testing format doesn't allow you to return to earlier questions, just make an educated guess; then put it out of your mind and move on.

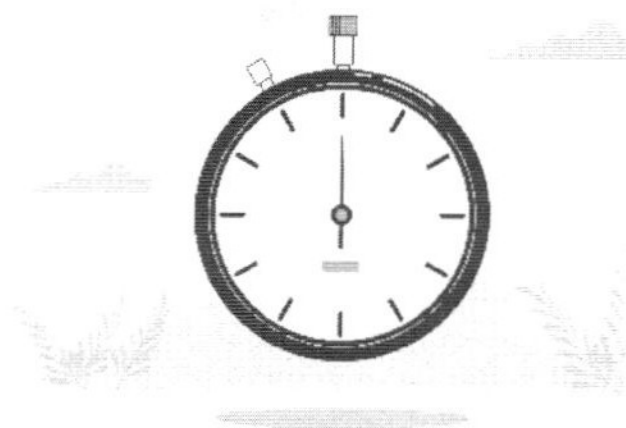

On the easier questions, be careful not to rush. It may seem wise to hurry through them so you have more time for the challenging ones, but it's not worth missing one if you know the concept and just didn't take the time to read the question fully. Work efficiently but make sure you understand the question and have looked at all of the answer choices, since more than one may seem right at first.

Even if you're paying attention to the time, you may find yourself a little behind at some point. You should speed up to get back on track, but do so wisely. Don't panic; just take a few seconds less on each question until you're caught up. Don't guess without thinking, but do look through the answer choices and eliminate any you know are wrong. If you can get down to two choices, it is often worthwhile to guess from those. Once you've chosen an answer, move on and don't dwell on any that you skipped or had to hurry through. If a question was taking too long, chances are it was one of the harder ones, so you weren't as likely to get it right anyway.

On the other hand, if you find yourself getting ahead of schedule, it may be beneficial to slow down a little. The more quickly you work, the more likely you are to make a careless mistake that will affect your score. You've budgeted time for each question, so don't be afraid to spend that time. Practice an efficient but careful pace to get the most out of the time you have.

Secret Key #5 – Have a Plan for Guessing

When you're taking the test, you may find yourself stuck on a question. Some of the answer choices seem better than others, but you don't see the one answer choice that is obviously correct. What do you do?

The scenario described above is very common, yet most test takers have not effectively prepared for it. Developing and practicing a plan for guessing may be one of the single most effective uses of your time as you get ready for the exam.

In developing your plan for guessing, there are three questions to address:

- When should you start the guessing process?
- How should you narrow down the choices?
- Which answer should you choose?

When to Start the Guessing Process

Unless your plan for guessing is to select C every time (which, despite its merits, is not what we recommend), you need to leave yourself enough time to apply your answer elimination strategies. Since you have a limited amount of time for each question, that means that if you're going to give yourself the best shot at guessing correctly, you have to decide quickly whether or not you will guess.

Of course, the best-case scenario is that you don't have to guess at all, so first, see if you can answer the question based on your knowledge of the subject and basic reasoning skills. Focus on the key words in the question and try to jog your memory of related topics. Give yourself a chance to bring the knowledge to mind, but once you realize that you don't have (or you can't access) the knowledge you need to answer the question, it's time to start the guessing process.

It's almost always better to start the guessing process too early than too late. It only takes a few seconds to remember something and answer the question from knowledge. Carefully eliminating wrong answer choices takes longer. Plus, going through the process of eliminating answer choices can actually help jog your memory.

Summary: Start the guessing process as soon as you decide that you can't answer the question based on your knowledge.

How to Narrow Down the Choices

The next chapter in this book (**Test-Taking Strategies**) includes a wide range of strategies for how to approach questions and how to look for answer choices to eliminate. You will definitely want to read those carefully, practice them, and figure out which ones work best for you. Here though, we're going to address a mindset rather than a particular strategy.

Your odds of guessing an answer correctly depend on how many options you are choosing from.

Number of options left	5	4	3	2	1
Odds of guessing correctly	20%	25%	33%	50%	100%

You can see from this chart just how valuable it is to be able to eliminate incorrect answers and make an educated guess, but there are two things that many test takers do that cause them to miss out on the benefits of guessing:

- Accidentally eliminating the correct answer
- Selecting an answer based on an impression

We'll look at the first one here, and the second one in the next section.

To avoid accidentally eliminating the correct answer, we recommend a thought exercise called **the $5 challenge**. In this challenge, you only eliminate an answer choice from contention if you are willing to bet $5 on it being wrong. Why $5? Five dollars is a small but not insignificant amount of money. It's an amount you could afford to lose but wouldn't want to throw away. And while losing $5 once might not hurt too much, doing it twenty times will set you back $100. In the same way, each small decision you make—eliminating a choice here, guessing on a question there—won't by itself impact your score very much, but when you put them all together, they can make a big difference. By holding each answer choice elimination decision to a higher standard, you can reduce the risk of accidentally eliminating the correct answer.

The $5 challenge can also be applied in a positive sense: If you are willing to bet $5 that an answer choice *is* correct, go ahead and mark it as correct.

Summary: Only eliminate an answer choice if you are willing to bet $5 that it is wrong.

Which Answer to Choose

You're taking the test. You've run into a hard question and decided you'll have to guess. You've eliminated all the answer choices you're willing to bet $5 on. Now you have to pick an answer. Why do we even need to talk about this? Why can't you just pick whichever one you feel like when the time comes?

The answer to these questions is that if you don't come into the test with a plan, you'll rely on your impression to select an answer choice, and if you do that, you risk falling into a trap. The test writers know that everyone who takes their test will be guessing on some of the questions, so they intentionally write wrong answer choices to seem plausible. You still have to pick an answer though, and if the wrong answer choices are designed to look right, how can you ever be sure that you're not falling for their trap? The best solution we've found to this dilemma is to take the decision out of your hands entirely. Here is the process we recommend:

Once you've eliminated any choices that you are confident (willing to bet $5) are wrong, select the first remaining choice as your answer.

Whether you choose to select the first remaining choice, the second, or the last, the important thing is that you use some preselected standard. Using this approach guarantees that you will not be enticed into selecting an answer choice that looks right, because you are not basing your decision on how the answer choices look.

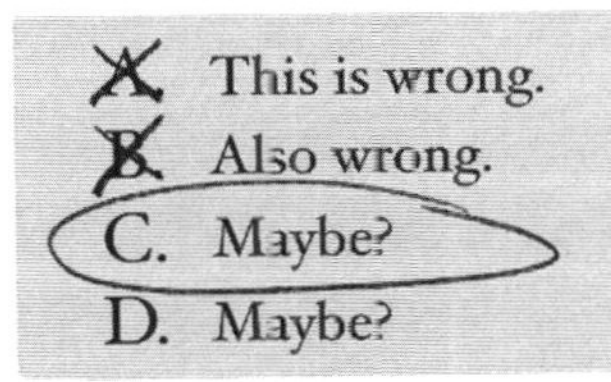

This is not meant to make you question your knowledge. Instead, it is to help you recognize the difference between your knowledge and your impressions. There's a huge difference between thinking an answer is right because of what you know, and thinking an answer is right because it looks or sounds like it should be right.

Summary: To ensure that your selection is appropriately random, make a predetermined selection from among all answer choices you have not eliminated.

Test-Taking Strategies

This section contains a list of test-taking strategies that you may find helpful as you work through the test. By taking what you know and applying logical thought, you can maximize your chances of answering any question correctly!

It is very important to realize that every question is different and every person is different: no single strategy will work on every question, and no single strategy will work for every person. That's why we've included all of them here, so you can try them out and determine which ones work best for different types of questions and which ones work best for you.

Question Strategies

✓ Read Carefully

Read the question and the answer choices carefully. Don't miss the question because you misread the terms. You have plenty of time to read each question thoroughly and make sure you understand what is being asked. Yet a happy medium must be attained, so don't waste too much time. You must read carefully and efficiently.

✓ Contextual Clues

Look for contextual clues. If the question includes a word you are not familiar with, look at the immediate context for some indication of what the word might mean. Contextual clues can often give you all the information you need to decipher the meaning of an unfamiliar word. Even if you can't determine the meaning, you may be able to narrow down the possibilities enough to make a solid guess at the answer to the question.

✓ Prefixes

If you're having trouble with a word in the question or answer choices, try dissecting it. Take advantage of every clue that the word might include. Prefixes can be a huge help. Usually, they allow you to determine a basic meaning. *Pre-* means before, *post-* means after, *pro-* is positive, *de-* is negative. From prefixes, you can get an idea of the general meaning of the word and try to put it into context.

✓ Hedge Words

Watch out for critical hedge words, such as *likely, may, can, often, almost, mostly, usually, generally, rarely,* and *sometimes.* Question writers insert these hedge phrases to cover every possibility. Often an answer choice will be wrong simply because it leaves no room for exception. Be on guard for answer choices that have definitive words such as *exactly* and *always.*

✓ Switchback Words

Stay alert for *switchbacks.* These are the words and phrases frequently used to alert you to shifts in thought. The most common switchback words are *but, although,* and *however.* Others include *nevertheless, on the other hand, even though, while, in spite of, despite,* and *regardless of.* Switchback words are important to catch because they can change the direction of the question or an answer choice.

☑ FACE VALUE

When in doubt, use common sense. Accept the situation in the problem at face value. Don't read too much into it. These problems will not require you to make wild assumptions. If you have to go beyond creativity and warp time or space in order to have an answer choice fit the question, then you should move on and consider the other answer choices. These are normal problems rooted in reality. The applicable relationship or explanation may not be readily apparent, but it is there for you to figure out. Use your common sense to interpret anything that isn't clear.

Answer Choice Strategies

☑ ANSWER SELECTION

The most thorough way to pick an answer choice is to identify and eliminate wrong answers until only one is left, then confirm it is the correct answer. Sometimes an answer choice may immediately seem right, but be careful. The test writers will usually put more than one reasonable answer choice on each question, so take a second to read all of them and make sure that the other choices are not equally obvious. As long as you have time left, it is better to read every answer choice than to pick the first one that looks right without checking the others.

☑ ANSWER CHOICE FAMILIES

An answer choice family consists of two (in rare cases, three) answer choices that are very similar in construction and cannot all be true at the same time. If you see two answer choices that are direct opposites or parallels, one of them is usually the correct answer. For instance, if one answer choice says that quantity *x* increases and another either says that quantity *x* decreases (opposite) or says that quantity *y* increases (parallel), then those answer choices would fall into the same family. An answer choice that doesn't match the construction of the answer choice family is more likely to be incorrect. Most questions will not have answer choice families, but when they do appear, you should be prepared to recognize them.

☑ ELIMINATE ANSWERS

Eliminate answer choices as soon as you realize they are wrong, but make sure you consider all possibilities. If you are eliminating answer choices and realize that the last one you are left with is also wrong, don't panic. Start over and consider each choice again. There may be something you missed the first time that you will realize on the second pass.

☑ AVOID FACT TRAPS

Don't be distracted by an answer choice that is factually true but doesn't answer the question. You are looking for the choice that answers the question. Stay focused on what the question is asking for so you don't accidentally pick an answer that is true but incorrect. Always go back to the question and make sure the answer choice you've selected actually answers the question and is not merely a true statement.

☑ EXTREME STATEMENTS

In general, you should avoid answers that put forth extreme actions as standard practice or proclaim controversial ideas as established fact. An answer choice that states the "process should be used in certain situations, if…" is much more likely to be correct than one that states the "process should be discontinued completely." The first is a calm rational statement and doesn't even make a definitive, uncompromising stance, using a hedge word *if* to provide wiggle room, whereas the second choice is far more extreme.

⊘ BENCHMARK

As you read through the answer choices and you come across one that seems to answer the question well, mentally select that answer choice. This is not your final answer, but it's the one that will help you evaluate the other answer choices. The one that you selected is your benchmark or standard for judging each of the other answer choices. Every other answer choice must be compared to your benchmark. That choice is correct until proven otherwise by another answer choice beating it. If you find a better answer, then that one becomes your new benchmark. Once you've decided that no other choice answers the question as well as your benchmark, you have your final answer.

⊘ PREDICT THE ANSWER

Before you even start looking at the answer choices, it is often best to try to predict the answer. When you come up with the answer on your own, it is easier to avoid distractions and traps because you will know exactly what to look for. The right answer choice is unlikely to be word-for-word what you came up with, but it should be a close match. Even if you are confident that you have the right answer, you should still take the time to read each option before moving on.

General Strategies

⊘ TOUGH QUESTIONS

If you are stumped on a problem or it appears too hard or too difficult, don't waste time. Move on! Remember though, if you can quickly check for obviously incorrect answer choices, your chances of guessing correctly are greatly improved. Before you completely give up, at least try to knock out a couple of possible answers. Eliminate what you can and then guess at the remaining answer choices before moving on.

⊘ CHECK YOUR WORK

Since you will probably not know every term listed and the answer to every question, it is important that you get credit for the ones that you do know. Don't miss any questions through careless mistakes. If at all possible, try to take a second to look back over your answer selection and make sure you've selected the correct answer choice and haven't made a costly careless mistake (such as marking an answer choice that you didn't mean to mark). This quick double check should more than pay for itself in caught mistakes for the time it costs.

⊘ PACE YOURSELF

It's easy to be overwhelmed when you're looking at a page full of questions; your mind is confused and full of random thoughts, and the clock is ticking down faster than you would like. Calm down and maintain the pace that you have set for yourself. Especially as you get down to the last few minutes of the test, don't let the small numbers on the clock make you panic. As long as you are on track by monitoring your pace, you are guaranteed to have time for each question.

⊘ DON'T RUSH

It is very easy to make errors when you are in a hurry. Maintaining a fast pace in answering questions is pointless if it makes you miss questions that you would have gotten right otherwise. Test writers like to include distracting information and wrong answers that seem right. Taking a little extra time to avoid careless mistakes can make all the difference in your test score. Find a pace that allows you to be confident in the answers that you select.

⊘ Keep Moving

Panicking will not help you pass the test, so do your best to stay calm and keep moving. Taking deep breaths and going through the answer elimination steps you practiced can help to break through a stress barrier and keep your pace.

Final Notes

The combination of a solid foundation of content knowledge and the confidence that comes from practicing your plan for applying that knowledge is the key to maximizing your performance on test day. As your foundation of content knowledge is built up and strengthened, you'll find that the strategies included in this chapter become more and more effective in helping you quickly sift through the distractions and traps of the test to isolate the correct answer.

Now that you're preparing to move forward into the test content chapters of this book, be sure to keep your goal in mind. As you read, think about how you will be able to apply this information on the test. If you've already seen sample questions for the test and you have an idea of the question format and style, try to come up with questions of your own that you can answer based on what you're reading. This will give you valuable practice applying your knowledge in the same ways you can expect to on test day.

Good luck and good studying!

Reading

Literature

Explicit Information

Explicit information includes facts and statements that are found directly in a passage or a story. It is not information that is hinted at or information you need to make a conclusion about. Explicit information may be found in many forms; it can be contained in a quote as well as in a description. It can be found in dialogue and in actions. This information can sometimes be used to support an inference. The answers to questions about explicit information are found through careful reading of the text. Attention is given to pertinent facts or other information. In fiction, details about characters, events, and setting can be both explicit and implicit.

Read the following excerpt and identify the information that is explicit.

> According to an ancient Greek legend, an inventor named Daedalus was imprisoned on an island by an angry king. His son, Icarus, was with him. The inventor came up with an escape plan. He created two pairs of wings from feathers and a wooden frame. He made one for himself and one for his son.

Explicit information is information found directly in the text. It is not inferred; it is not suggested. The explicit information in this excerpt is about the Greek myth that tells the story of the inventor Daedalus. The excerpt says that the inventor Daedalus and his son Icarus were imprisoned on an island by an angry king. It says that he had a plan of escape, and that he created two pairs of wings from feathers and a wooden frame. This information is found directly in the excerpt. It is not necessary to make any inferences or guesses to obtain this information.

Inference

An inference is a conclusion that a reader can make based on the facts and other information in a passage or a story. An inference is based both on what is found in a passage or a story and what is known from personal experience. For instance, a story may say that a character is frightened and that he can hear the sounds of wolves in the distance. Based on both what is in the text and personal knowledge, it might be a logical conclusion that the character is frightened because he hears the sound of wolves. A good inference is supported by the information in a passage. Inferences are different from explicit information, which is clearly stated in a passage. Inferences are not stated in a passage. A reader must put the information together to come up with a logical conclusion.

Read the excerpt and decide why Jana finally relaxed.

> Jana loved her job, but the work was very demanding. She had trouble relaxing. She called a friend, but she still thought about work. She ordered a pizza, but eating it did not help. Then her kitten jumped on her lap and began to purr. Jana leaned back and began to hum a little tune. She felt better.

You can draw the conclusion that Jana relaxes because her kitten jumped on her lap. The kitten purred, and Jana leaned back and hummed a tune. Then, she felt better. The excerpt does not explicitly say that this is the reason why she was able to relax. The text leaves the matter unclear. But, the reader can infer or make a "best guess" that this is the reason she is relaxing. This is a logical conclusion based on the information in the passage. It is the best conclusion a reader can make based on the information he or she has read. Inferences are based on the information in a passage, but they are not directly stated in the passage.

DETERMINING THE THEME OF A PASSAGE

The theme of a passage is what the reader learns from the text or the passage. It is the lesson or moral contained in the passage. A passage can have two or more themes that convey its overall idea. The theme or themes of a passage are often based on universal themes. They can frequently be expressed using well-known sayings about life, society, or human nature, such as "Hard work pays off" or "Good triumphs over evil." Themes are not usually stated explicitly. The reader must figure them out by carefully reading the passage. Themes are often the reason why passages are written; they give a passage unity and meaning. Themes are created through plot development. The events of a story help shape the themes of a passage.

EXPLAIN WHY "TAKE CARE OF WHAT YOU CARE ABOUT" ACCURATELY DESCRIBES THE THEME OF THE FOLLOWING EXCERPT.

> Luca collected baseball cards. But, Luca wasn't very careful with them. He left them around the house. His dog liked to chew. Luca and his friend Bart were looking at his collection. Then, they went outside. When Luca got home, he saw his dog chewing on his cards. They were ruined.

This excerpt tells the story of a boy who is careless with his baseball cards and leaves them lying around. His dog ends up chewing them and ruining them. The lesson is that if you care about something, you need to take care of it. This is the point of the story. The theme is the lesson that a story teaches. Some stories have more than one theme, but this is not really true of this excerpt. The reader needs to figure out the theme based on what happens in the story. Sometimes, as in the case of fables, the theme is stated directly in the text. However, this is not usually the case.

COMPONENTS OF A STORY SUMMARY

A summary of a passage or a story should include the main ideas of a passage and also the important details that support the main ideas. It shouldn't just be a general statement about what a passage is about, but should include important events and other details that make the story what it is. In order to write an objective summary, you have to reflect on what the passage is about. A summary puts the information in a concise form. Consequently, summarizing is different from paraphrasing. Paraphrasing involves rewording the main idea and supporting ideas in a fairly detailed way; summarizing does not. Summaries afford the reader the opportunity to quickly review the main points of a passage and the important details.

SETTING AND CHARACTERS

Without characters and setting, there is no story. They affect the plot of a story in many ways. The setting creates the background for the action. The setting could be someplace exotic or mundane, but wherever it is, it creates limitations for the characters. Characters are also essential to a story. They bring the story to life; it is their decisions, what they do, and how they act that creates the plot of a story and ultimately its theme. Characters can have good traits and bad traits. Analyzing what these are based on what a character does and says is an important aspect of comprehending the meaning of a story.

READ THE EXCERPT AND EXPLAIN HOW THE SETTING INFLUENCES THE PLOT.

> The cave was dark, so dark that Ernesto could not see a thing. He could not see his hand in front of him. He was lost, and he knew that time was running out. He could hear the trickle of water somewhere in the distance. He knew he had to follow the sound. It was his only hope of escaping.

The setting of the cave creates a conflict since Ernesto cannot see a thing and is lost. The excerpt also says that Ernesto's time is running out. While the reader does not know why this is the case, this increases the tension in the story. The fact that Ernesto can hear the dripping of the water is also important to the plot, since it influences the events of the story. Ernesto decides he should go towards the sound of the water. Setting influences the plot here because it creates a struggle for the main character. It also influences the character since Ernesto makes choices about what he should do based on the setting.

Impact of the Order of a Story or Introduction of Characters Has on a Story

The way in which an author chooses to order the events of or introduce characters in a story has a strong effect on it. Most stories are told in chronological order; one event occurs after another. But, an author can influence the development of a story by placing one event out of order to emphasize its importance. Another technique used by some authors is a flashback, in which time changes from the present to the past. When it comes to introducing characters, authors have a great deal of latitude. Authors often introduce the most important characters first so that the reader will have time to get acquainted with the characters' past and present situations. Readers are often influenced by the author's feelings toward a particular character, which often have an effect on how a character is introduced.

Determining the Meaning of Words or Phrases as They Are Used in a Text

When the reader does not understand a word or a phrase that is used in a passage or a story, it is important to examine the context clues around the word or phrase that provide hints about its meaning. Many words have more than one meaning, and it is only through an examination of the context that the reader can figure out the correct meaning. The word "crown" is a good example. This word has several meanings, including a coronet, the top of a head, the act of awarding something to someone, or even the act of hitting someone. Therefore, it is important to understand the context. In the sentence, "He sought to be crowned the winner of the competition," it is clear that the meaning is "to be awarded." Context must also be used to determine the meaning of phrases. In the sentence, "He wasn't going to stand for that anymore, so he told his boss off," the reader can use context to get a sense of the meaning of "going to stand for." In this case, the phrase means "not put up with."

Figurative Use of a Word

Authors use literary devices like figurative language to expand reality in a vivid way. An author can utilize figurative language to connect things in an exaggerated way, which results in a stronger, more vivid image. Examples of figurative language include simile, metaphor, personification, and hyperbole. Similes compare things using the comparing words *like* or *as*. "She is as brave as a lion" is an example of a simile. Metaphors compare things without using comparing words. An example of a metaphor is "She is a lion in the wild." Personification attributes human traits to an animal or non-living thing. "Time flew by" is an example of personification. Hyperbole is an exaggeration that is not believable. "He waited in line for years" is an example of this literary device.

Read the excerpt; identify the form of figurative language represented by the phrase "like a fresh April shower," and explain your answer.

> We had been sequestered inside the barn all afternoon. It was hot, really hot. When the sun finally set and I opened the door, the evening air swept over us like a fresh April shower, leaving us ready to enjoy the evening.

The phrase "like a fresh April shower" is an example of a simile. The phrase compares the air with a fresh April shower and uses the word "like," so it qualifies as a simile. Similes compare two things using the word "like" or "as." This phrase is not a metaphor. Although it compares two things, it uses the word "like"; metaphors do not use either "like" or "as" to compare two things. It is not an example of personification, because nothing is being given human traits. There is no sign of hyperbole here either; there is no sense of an exaggeration.

Relationship Between the Denotative and Connotative Meaning of Words

The denotative meaning of a word and the connotative meaning are only alike in that, according to the dictionary, they mean the same thing. However, that is where the similarities end. The connotative meaning of a word is what is suggested above and beyond the literal meaning. For instance, the word "untidy" might mean "messy" or "unclean," whereas the word "slovenly" suggests something closer to "filthy." When writers create stories, they frequently use words that have strong connotations to describe and develop the characters and the setting. It is important for the reader to analyze these word choices to gain a better understanding of the author's purpose.

Read the following sentence.

I expected my gear to be inspected, but I never thought it would be scrutinized to this degree.

Explain the connotative meanings of the word "scrutinized" and how they relate to the word "inspected."

Both "scrutinized" and "inspected" have the dictionary meaning of being "closely looked at" or "studied." But, the word "scrutinized" means that something is being dissected and analyzed, not just inspected or checked out. The word "scrutinized" is a much stronger term than the word "inspected." Many things are inspected, but not everything is scrutinized. It is important to choose words that fit the situation, something that is done in this sentence. The connotations that a word brings to a sentence will impact the way a reader comprehends what is being written about. Words with strong connotations help a reader get a feel for what is being written about.

Impact of Words on Tone

Words can have a large impact on the tone of a passage. Tone is a result of the choice of language. For instance, when talking about or suggesting the mood of a person or a setting, it is vital to choose the right language to describe it. Is a person ecstatic, or is the person simply content? Is a room barren, or is it just empty? Similarly, using strong action verbs can create a tone that is forceful and remembered easily. The verb *buttress*, for instance, has a much stronger impact than the verb *strengthen*. Even though both words have basically the same meaning, the first one creates a more vivid image in the mind of the reader. It is important to use words that will be understood by the audience and will have the desired effect.

Fresh and Engaging Language

One way to get a reader's attention and hold it is to use language that is fresh and engaging. Using a personal point of view is a good way to accomplish this. You should try to generate excitement by using a different perspective. Always avoid clichés—they will come across as stale and worn out. Learning editing skills is useful; it will help you eliminate unnecessary portions of a text. Use a dictionary and a thesaurus to locate the words you are looking for, and analyze the words to determine how a reader might perceive them. Finally, read your passage aloud to see how it sounds.

Read the excerpt. Describe why the language is fresh and engaging.

"Full many a glorious morning have I seen
Flatter the mountain tops with sovereign eye,
Kissing with golden face the meadows green,
Gilding pale streams with heavenly alchemy;"
(Shakespeare, Sonnet XXXIII)

In these few lines, Shakespeare provides the reader with a fresh, new image of nature Morning is personified as a romantic king in love with the meadows and streams. It is not just any morning, but *a glorious morning*, and it makes the mountain tops look even better than usual. Alchemy was a combination of magic and science thought to enable the creation of precious gold from ordinary metals, and the excerpt describes the streams as gilded, or covered with gold. The king himself is *kissing with golden face.* The lines are simple, and at the same time, sweet and poetic. The sun is the ruler of all. The writing is fresh and engaging.

Comedic or Tragic Resolution

When an author decides to include a comedic or tragic resolution in a story, the author is using a time-tested literary form that has existed for hundreds, even thousands, of years. The tragedy has a strict format. There is a tragic hero or protagonist who has a fatal flaw and becomes victim to it in the end. The play or story always ends sadly, with the hero in most cases dying or coming to some terrible end. A comedic resolution, on the other hand, always includes a happy ending. There are playful aspects to the plot and the ways in which the characters interact. These literary forms tell the reader what to expect in the story and how to assess the plot. They act as signposts as a reader proceeds through a text.

Understatement or a Sense of Irony

Many authors enjoy using a sense of irony or understatement as they write a story. Both techniques distance the writer from the characters and the events of a story. In either case, the reader must read between the lines to figure out what the author is actually getting at and what his or her point of view actually is. Understatement can be used as a humorous vehicle, allowing the author to comment on what is happening without being deeply emotionally invested in it. Irony allows the author to make a statement about what is really occurring without openly stating it. When reading a text, be sure to look for any underlying meaning that an author might be trying to convey. An initial reading of a text may not be enough to discern its true intended meaning. The way an author talks about what is happening often conveys that author's viewpoint of the events.

Satire vs. Sarcasm

Satire exposes the follies, foibles, and traditions of society, and is often humorous. A satire critiques the pretensions of powerful people in society. While criticism is intended, it is not overt, but rather implied. Mark Twain often employed satire to make a comment about the society in which his characters lived. Sarcasm is a type of humor that is meant to be insulting. Satire may employ the literary technique of irony, which is the tension between what is expected and what actually happens. Sarcasm is a sharp, bitter comment or remark that may or may not utilize understatement. It is an obvious criticism, and does not have the sophistication or creativity of satire, which is usually associated with an entire work. Sarcasm is usually limited to a comment.

Distinguishing Between an Author's Point of View and What They May Say Literarily About a Character or a Situation

An author may use a wide array of literary techniques to discuss a topic, a character, or a situation, which could disguise the author's real feelings regarding what he or she is writing about. For instance, a writer might say that an area received a "little rain," when in fact the land might be flooded with water. Or, an author could describe a dent as "a little scratch" when there is actually an enormous dent. A reader must be able to put a writer's words into perspective to determine what has actually occurred.

The same is true when a writer uses irony to make a comment. Consider the following sentence: "I have little doubt that you will receive the praise that you deserve for your hard work." Taken at face value, this would be a compliment. However, if the situation is such that the recipient of the comment has made a complete fool of himself, the comment becomes irony, because the opposite of what is being said is true. Here again, the reader has to be careful to examine a situation described by a writer before jumping to conclusions about the author's viewpoint.

WAYS IN WHICH SHAKESPEARE'S *ROMEO AND JULIET* IS A TIMELESS STORY

The story of a young man and woman falling in love and coming to a tragic end has been told over and over, and it represents a universal theme in literature. It was originally told by the Roman writer Ovid in his play *Pyramus and Thisbe*, which is a story of forbidden love. In modern times, a musical with a plot similar to *Romeo and Juliet* is *West Side Story*, which was in fact based on Shakespeare's play. It's important to note, however, that the theme was explored even before Shakespeare wrote his tragedy. Universal themes are found throughout literature. Even the Disney movie *Lady and the Tramp* has elements of the story of ill-fated love that is recounted in *Romeo and Juliet*.

> In what way is *Antigone* by the Greek writer Sophocles related to Henry David Thoreau's essay "Civil Disobedience"? In *Antigone*, the title character defies Creon, the ruler of Thebes, by invoking divine justice and breaking Creon's law to bury her brother. In his essay, Thoreau argues that people have a right and responsibility to rebel against laws that are immoral.

They are related because they share a universal theme of rebelliousness against laws that are unjust. Much of literature contains universal themes that repeat situations and ideals that humans live by. The fact that Antigone went against Creon shows that she had moral courage; the same is true of Thoreau, who argued against laws that were unjust. Even though *Antigone* is a play and was written long ago, it still relates to Thoreau's essay, which was written in the 19th century. Universal themes are timeless and are often repeated, but the context in which they are presented is affected by the times in which they are written.

BOTH HENRY DAVID THOREAU AND NATHANIEL HAWTHORNE WERE AMERICAN WRITERS OF THE 19TH CENTURY. THOREAU'S ESSAYS FOCUSED ON THE QUIET DESPERATION OF MAN. HAWTHORNE'S NOVELS FOCUSED ON CHARACTERS WHO WERE STRUGGLING WITH THE PURITANICAL BACKGROUND OF AMERICA. DISCUSS THE WAYS IN WHICH THEIR VIEWPOINTS WERE DIFFERENT.

Thoreau was part of the Transcendental Movement that was awakening during the 19th century. It held that nature was a vital part of the human experience. Unlike the Puritanical viewpoint that people had little control over their destiny, the Transcendentalists believed that humans could choose their destiny. Thoreau was writing from this viewpoint, while Hawthorne was more concerned with the Puritanical legacy, which allowed little room for change or imagination. His books were a comment on this strict background, while Thoreau's essays were an exploration of a new world. Even though they wrote during the same century, their works represented different understandings of man's position in the universe.

UPTON SINCLAIR'S NOVEL THE JUNGLE IS ABOUT AN IMMIGRANT FAMILY'S EXPERIENCES WORKING IN A FACTORY; JOHN STEINBECK'S NOVEL THE GRAPES OF WRATH IS ABOUT A FAMILY OF MIGRANT WORKERS SUFFERING IN THE DUST BOWL OF MIDDLE AMERICA. THEY WERE BOTH WRITTEN IN THE EARLY 20TH CENTURY. DISCUSS WHY THESE AUTHORS MOST LIKELY DECIDED TO WRITE ABOUT THESE SUBJECTS.

These authors wrote about poor people in difficult situations; they were both concerned about social problems. This is a common theme of early 20th century literature, when the concept of helping the poor worker was just being introduced. One writer spoke of an immigrant family. The other based his novel on a migrant family. They would have had a lot in common, since both families were without roots. This theme is typical of the literature of the early 20th century, when so many immigrants were pouring into the United States. It was also timely because there were few laws restricting the kind of work that migrants could do

Importance of Being Able to Read and Comprehend a Wide Variety of Texts by the End of Grade 11 and Grade 12

It is important for an 11th grader to be able to read and comprehend literature—including stories, dramas, and poetry—in order to be well-versed in literature and how it reflects the various periods in which it was written. The student will develop a good background in the cultural aspects of writing, and will know how to respond to cultural references found in texts. The ability to read and comprehend literature will also help the student prepare for his or her future academic and career path.

The reasons why it is important for a student to be able to comprehend a wide variety of texts by the end of the 12th grade are manifold. This background will give the student a great advantage in terms of achieving success in school and the business world. Being widely read ensures greater knowledge of the world, helps a student become well-versed in cultural differences, and also gives the student a chance to develop his or her vocabulary and ability to express her or himself. Ultimately, having read a large number of different literary books will educate the student in many fields, and will help her or him become confident in our ever-complicated world, where communication is vital.

Informational Texts

Inference

An inference is a conclusion you can make based on the evidence in a passage. For instance, if a passage says that there are many people who ride bicycles to work, and that many people prefer riding a bike to driving a car, you might make the conclusion that riding a bike is fun. This is based on the information that you have on hand; it could be wrong, but it is the best guess you can make. Inferences need to have evidence that they are the most likely outcome. In this case, the fact that many people prefer riding a bike to work over driving a car leads the reader to conclude that riding a bike is fun.

Identify the Information in the Following Excerpt That Supports the Inference That Aluminum Is a Good Material for a Boat.

> Cement is heavy, and it can support weight. But, it sinks in water. Aluminum is light, and it does not rust easily. It floats easily. Bricks are made up of clay that is fired. They are fire resistant, and they last a long time. But, bricks are heavy.

The information that supports the inference that aluminum is a good material for a boat is that it is light and does not rust easily. Another supporting detail is that it floats easily. This is what the excerpt says. And this is the kind of evidence that is needed to support the inference identified in the question. The other details describe other materials, but they do not give information that suggests these materials would be good for a boat. Inferences are the best conclusions that can be made based on the information at hand.

Determining the Central Ideas of a Passage

Central ideas are what a passage is mainly about. They are why the passage is written. The main idea is often found in a topic sentence or even a concluding sentence, and there are supporting details found in the passage that expand upon the main idea. There can, however, be more than one central idea, and these main ideas can be related and intertwined. For instance, the main or central idea of a passage may be that rainforests are drying out. A related main idea might be that the result of rainforest destruction is a loss of wildlife. These two central ideas are obviously related, and the passage may present both of them by focusing on one in one part of the passage and the other in another part of the passage. Another way they could be related is in a cause and effect relationship, with the loss of rainforests being the reason for losses of wildlife. It is important to always check to see if there is more than one central idea in a passage.

READ THE EXCERPT BELOW. IDENTIFY AND DISCUSS THE MAIN IDEA.

> Students who have jobs while attending high school tend not to have as much time to complete their homework as other students. They also do not have time for other activities. We should try to persuade our young people to concentrate on doing well in school, not to concentrate on making money. Having a job while you are a student is harmful.

The main idea of the excerpt is actually the last sentence: "Having a job while you are a student is harmful." This is what the excerpt is mostly about. The other sentences contain supporting information: students who have jobs don't have as much time for homework; students with jobs don't have time for as many activities. These are both supporting details that tell more about the main idea. The third sentence deals with a persuasive argument; it is another kind of detail. Only the last sentence tells what the excerpt is mostly about. Main ideas are sometimes found in a topic sentence at the start of a text or in the concluding sentence, which is the case in this excerpt.

SUMMARY OF AN INFORMATIONAL TEXT

A summary of an informational text should include the main idea or ideas of the passage and also the pertinent supporting details. A summary should not be a vague statement about what a passage is about, but should include important facts, events, or evidence that make the text a complete work. In order to write an objective summary, you need to think about what the text is saying, and then create a precise outline of the main idea and the important supporting information. Summarizing is not the same as paraphrasing. Paraphrasing involves rewording the main idea and supporting ideas in a fairly detailed way; summarizing does not. Summaries afford the reader the opportunity to quickly review the main points of a passage and the important details.

ANALYZING A TEXT

When you read a text, you need to pay attention. You need to watch for the introduction of ideas. You need to figure out how the ideas that are introduced are developed. When you read a complex text, it may be difficult to follow. Sometimes, it is hard to understand how one idea is linked to another idea. Sometimes, it helps to make an outline of a text. This will help you identify the main ideas. Then, you can figure out which ideas are supporting details. A complex text may also have vocabulary that you cannot understand. If you cannot figure out the meaning of certain words from the context, you can make a list of these words. Then, look them up in a dictionary. This will help you understand the meaning of the text.

Even an informational text tells a story. It introduces information, ideas, individuals, or events, and then provides details about them. A careful reader must learn to figure out the relationships between the details that an author includes and the ideas that the author introduced earlier in the text. Some of the information that is added may be used to supplement the description of an individual, an event, or an idea. Other information may be used to criticize an event, an idea, or an individual. It is up to the reader to have a discerning eye and decide what direction an author is taking by analyzing the author's language and viewpoint, as well as other information.

Meaning of Words and Phrases

The meaning of words and phrases can typically be determined from the context of the sentence in which they appear, as well as the surrounding sentences. It may be necessary to read an entire text to figure out the meaning of a term, particularly a technical or legal term. While words may be used in a literal manner, phrases can be more difficult to figure out since their meaning is often not tied to the exact meaning of the words that comprise them. Phrases are often expressions that need to be interpreted. Expressions are idioms that are usually part of the vernacular of a language. They may require more effort to understand, although the meaning can often still be gleaned from the context.

Discuss the meaning of the phrase "jump ship" in the following sentence.

> The start-up company wasn't working out the way that Hal and his partner hoped, and they thought it was time to jump ship and get into another business.

To figure out the meaning of the phrase "jump ship," the reader needs to look for context clues in the same way he or she would to figure out the meaning of a single word. The sentence says that the start-up company wasn't working out. It says that Hal and his partner thought it was time to get into another business. You can tell from the context of the sentence that the expression "jump ship" means to get out of something or to quit something. It has nautical overtones, and it comes from a nautical saying, but the context of the sentence makes it clear what the expression, or idiom, means. Although it might seem to have negative connotations, it does not necessarily have to be negative. It is a kind of final act, which could be construed as negative. However, the context of the sentence suggests that "jumping ship" in this instance might result in something positive occurring.

Read the excerpt below. Use the context clues to decide what the word "Waterloo" means in this instance.

> Connie was worried that the competition was her Waterloo. She realized she wasn't Napoleon and she wasn't losing her entire kingdom because she lost a battle, but that's how it felt to her.

Using context clues is a good way to figure out the meanings of words and expressions without having to look them up in a dictionary. The way to discover context clues is to study the text. The excerpt says that Connie was worried that the competition was her Waterloo. This is obviously a reference to something, but it takes further analysis to figure out what it means. The next sentence talks about Napoleon and how he lost a kingdom because of a battle. One can draw the conclusion that "Waterloo" was probably the battle, and that someone's Waterloo is something that a person loses or does badly in. This helps the reader figure out the meaning of the word.

Figurative Language

Figurative language is language that is used in a non-literal way. It allows the writer to expand the ways in which he or she uses language, making it more colorful and fresh. Figurative language takes a word or an expression that has a literal meaning and gives it a new one. For instance, an author might say that Lilli is like a graceful swan. While everyone knows that Lilli is a person, the image of Lilli as a graceful swan casts a new descriptive meaning. Figurative language takes many forms; it can be in the form of a simile, a metaphor, personification, or hyperbole. Similes compare things using the comparing words "*like*" or "*as*." An example is, "Lilli is like a graceful swan." Metaphors compare things without using comparing words. An example is, "Lilli is a swan when she moves." Personification attributes human traits to an animal or an inanimate object. An example is, "The swan spoke to Lilli."

Read the excerpt from former President George W. Bush's Second Inaugural Address.

> "...By our efforts, we have lit a fire as well - a fire in the minds of men. It warms those who feel its power, it burns those who fight its progress, and one day this untamed fire of freedom will reach the darkest corners of our world."

Discuss the metaphor that former President Bush uses in this excerpt.

The metaphor that President Bush uses is that of a fire of freedom that will grow in the minds of men and will warm those who feel its power. This fire is powerful, according to the metaphor, since it would burn those who fight against freedom. It is also powerful because it will reach all over the world. Bush uses the metaphor of a fire since it suggests light, and democracy is a kind of light that allows people to see the truth. That is why the metaphor is a powerful one. This is an example of how strong a metaphor can be in terms of getting a person's viewpoint and thoughts across to the public.

Aggressive vs. Assertive Connotations

The words "aggressive" and "assertive" both describe someone with a strong nature. However, the word "aggressive" suggests someone who may be hostile or belligerent, while the term "assertive" could be interpreted to mean self-confident or self-assured. "Aggressive" has negative connotations when used to describe someone's nature, while the word "assertive" has more positive connotations. These words are examples of differences in connotations, since they both have meanings that go beyond what appears in the dictionary. Words like these should be chosen carefully, since they can convey a message about someone that may or may not be intended. When choosing words, a writer needs to look for the most accurate word to describe a person or a thing.

Author's Point of View

When an author writes a text, he or she must choose the structure that will work best for the text. For informational passages, there are several different structures an author can use. These include question and answer order, chronological or sequential order, problem and solution order, cause and effect order, and spatial order. Some texts use a combination of two or more of these structures depending on the breakdown of the topic. For persuasive documents, a question and answer order is often a good choice because it allows for a dramatic presentation of materials. This structure allows the author to highlight arguments for or against a position. A cause and effect order structure might also be a good choice for a persuasive text, and would also allow for the highlighting of arguments, as would a problem and solution order. Compare and contrast and order of importance are reasonable choices for informational pieces, and possibly for persuasive texts as well. Chronological ordering would be more suitable for an informational piece on a person or an event, where the points that are being made are not meant to convince the reader of something. The author should choose the structure that will best meet his or her writing goals.

Veronica is doing a report on why people should stop the killing of whales. She is trying to figure out which text structure would best help her meet her goal to outline the reasons why this harvesting will result in the loss of species that are important to the environment. Describe which type of order would probably work best for this report, and explain why.

The best possible choices for the report would probably be either a problem and solution or a cause and effect organization, since they would allow the author to lay out the problem and the consequences of the killing of whales. A cause and effect order would show the immediate relationship between the killing of whales and its consequence; a problem and solution order would probably be best if the author wants to concentrate on the ways in which this practice is causing society problems and how the practice could be resolved. A compare and contrast structure would probably not work in this type of report. Finally, a chronological structure, which might be useful in part of the report to outline the past history of the practice, would probably not be a suitable structure for the entire report.

An author's point of view may be clear, or it may be hidden. It is important to read a text closely to find out exactly what the author thinks about the event, person, topic, or issue he or she is writing about. When reading, look for clues to the author's viewpoint in the form of emotional statements or critiques of others discussing the topic. Some authors make their viewpoints known only through rhetorical statements. These need to be analyzed closely to see if they should be taken at face value or if the author is somehow using rhetoric to exaggerate a point or to try to persuade the reader of something. Rhetoric can be a very effective vehicle that can draw a reader in through the use of elegant language. This is precisely why it is important to analyze an author's rhetoric to determine why he or she is employing it and what his or her goal might be. It is also vital to read the entire text before making any assumptions about an author's viewpoint.

THE PURPOSE OF THE RHETORIC IN THE FOLLOWING EXCERPT FROM A SPEECH BY FORMER PRESIDENT GEORGE W. BUSH.

> "Our opportunities are too great, our lives too short, to waste this moment. So tonight we vow to our nation. We will seize this moment of American promise. We will use these good times for great goals."

The President's purpose is clear; he wants to set an important goal for the public. In doing so, he is attempting to paint a picture of the importance of what he is saying. Phrases such as "Our opportunities are too great," "We will seize the moment," and "good times for great goals" set the stage for putting forth the President's agenda, which he hopes to present in the best possible light Words have the capacity to transfix listeners with their elegance, a fact clearly illustrated by this excerpt. That is why speeches are so important to the political arena, and it is why excellent speech writers are extremely important to political candidates.

USING INFORMATION TECHNOLOGY SKILLS WISELY

Good information technology skills are necessary in order to sift through the enormous amount of information available on just about any topic. Before beginning any research, ask yourself how much information you think you are going to need; think about your target audience and their needs. Utilize search engines to make the task go faster. When evaluating multiple sources of information, do not rely solely on how recent they are. Consider the validity of sources as well. Do not rely on just one source. Using digital media is important because it allows you to broaden your scope beyond just words to include graphics and charts. Take the time to understand what online sources of information are available, which ones are most appropriate, and how they support one another.

USING THE REASONING THAT THE FOUNDING FATHERS BELIEVED THAT AFRICAN AMERICANS COULD NOT BE VIEWED AS CITIZENS AS DEFINED IN THE US CONSTITUTION, AND THEREFORE HAD NO RIGHTS BEFORE THE COURT, CHIEF JUSTICE TANEY'S MAJORITY OPINION IGNITED A FIRESTORM OF CONTROVERSY IN THE ALREADY HEATED DEBATE BETWEEN PRO- AND ANTI-SLAVERY ADVOCATES IN THE UNITED STATES DURING THE MID-19TH CENTURY. MANY OPPONENTS DECRIED THE CHIEF JUSTICE'S RULING AS ONE THAT WAS MOTIVATED BY POLITICS. ONE RESULT WAS THAT THE US CONGRESS COULD NO LONGER REGULATE SLAVERY ANYWHERE. THE DRED SCOTT DECISION IS VIEWED AS ONE OF A SERIES OF EVENTS THAT EVENTUALLY PUSHED THE COUNTRY INTO THE CIVIL WAR.

ANALYZE THE FOLLOWING EXCERPT FROM LINCOLN'S SECOND INAUGURAL ADDRESS IN 1865.

> "It may seem strange that any men should dare to ask a just God's assistance in wringing their bread from the sweat of other men's faces, but let us judge not, that we be not judged. The prayers of both could not be answered. That of neither has been answered fully..."

In this excerpt and in the address, Lincoln is talking about slavery. Like the majority of people of his time, Lincoln learned to read by studying the Bible. He makes frequent references to the Bible, and he often uses the rhetoric of the Bible to drive his point home. This is common in 19th century literary documents. When he says, "Wringing their bread from the sweat of other men's faces," he is paraphrasing from the Book of Genesis, which refers to physical work. Here, the word *bread* is used to refer to the wealth of the slave owners. Lincoln finds it strange that these slave owners should pray to the same God as those who do not own slaves for assistance in making money. He encourages his audience not to be hypocritical when he says, "let us judge not." This is a reference to the Book of Matthew of the Bible.

Importance of Being a Proficient Reader of Literary Nonfiction Texts by Grade 11 and Grade 12

It is extremely important for a student to be proficient in reading literary nonfiction texts by the end of grade 11. These types of texts will play a key role in the student's future life (and success). In other words, the ability to comprehend language and vocabulary will help the student attain the academic level he or she hopes to or the type of employment desired. In all walks of life, people need to be able to read and comprehend a variety of materials. This is why the ability to understand literary nonfiction texts is a valuable tool. It is especially important for those who hope to do well on college entrance examinations as well as other kinds of job examinations.

It is of the utmost importance for a 12th-grade student to be able to read literary nonfiction proficiently. Not only is it important for future academic endeavors (e.g., college and graduate school), but it is also vital to future career success. Whether it is reading a newspaper, an employee manual, or a science text, it is crucial that a person be comfortable when reading and be able to comprehend the material without extreme effort. Without this ability, a person will face limitations in his or her academia and business life. Communication is extremely important in today's workplace, and the foundation of this skill is being able to comprehend reading materials.

Universal Themes Found in Literature Are Affected by the Time in Which the Literature Was Written

While universal themes are the same in terms of their meaning and what they depict or teach, the ways in which they are presented are affected by the time in which a literary piece was written. The characters and situations that are portrayed will mirror the environment in which the writer lived. Ancient literature depicts a time when myth was very much alive, and when the concept of personal freedom was still evolving and not taken for granted.

Evaluate the Purpose of the Following Excerpt from George Washington's Farewell Address, Which Was Given on September 19, 1796.

> "The unity of government which constitutes you one people is also now dear to you. It is justly so, for it is a main pillar in the edifice of your real independence, the support of your tranquility at home, your peace abroad; of your safety; of your prosperity; of that very liberty which you so highly prize..."

This address given by the first president of the US when he announced that he did not want to run for re-election went over the groundwork that had established the new country. The passage stresses *the unity of government which constitutes you one people.* Washington truly believed that the US would be able to survive any attack, from without as well as from within, if it stayed with this principle. There is a hint that Washington foresaw the difficulties of holding together *the main pillar* (the different states) that were to come. His farewell address would go on to influence politicians and leaders for many years to come.

Writing

Clear and Coherent Writing

Clear and coherent writing requires good initial planning. You need to determine what you are going to say, who you are saying it to, and how you want to say it, as well as the kind of tone you want to project. In the process of writing, organize your arguments and use a logical order to develop them. Use paragraph breaks to help organize your thoughts. Your sentences should be precise and to the point. Make sure your punctuation is correct. Your ideas should be supported by evidence, and opposing ideas should be mentioned as well. When you get to your conclusion, avoid being repetitious; concentrate on summarizing. Proofread what you have written to check for any errors; reading the text aloud is often helpful.

Importance of Planning, Revising, Editing, and Reviewing a Text

Draw up a brief plan before you start to write so that you know what points you are going to cover. Once you have finished the writing, it is a good idea to set it aside for a time. That way, when you look at it again to see if revisions are needed, you will be approaching it with a fresh mind. During the process of editing, make sure you check for any grammatical, spelling, punctuation, or usage errors. Are your supporting details clear and presented in a logical order? Will your audience respond to your text? During your review process, you may feel that some sections need to be rewritten. Think about whatever criticism your peers or adults may have had about previous work as you review your writing.

Read the following passage, explain why it needs to be revised, and discuss how best to revise it.

> Raising a puppy is more difficult. We all know how cute they are. Like kittens, they need a lot of care. So, don't be shocked that I tell you kittens are more cute.

The writer of these sentences has not made it clear what he or she is really trying to say. There is no organization, and there are grammatical and usage errors. A good revision would look like this:

> We all know how cute puppies and kittens are. They both require a lot of care, but I think puppies are more difficult to raise than kittens. I also think that kittens are cuter than puppies.

Here the thoughts are put down in a logical order. The writer makes a statement of fact (*puppies and kittens are cute*), and one of opinion (*I think...*), so it is clear what her preferences are. The passage now makes sense, and the writing is free from errors.

Conducting a Research Project

When conducting a short or a sustained research project to answer a question or solve a problem, it is a good idea to draw up a plan first. Then, make a list of keywords related to the question or problem. You can utilize these words either in a search engine or an online or print encyclopedia. Back issues of magazines, journals, and newspapers can also be used as source material. If you are synthesizing multiple sources, combine the similarities or the differences you have come up with. It is important that none of the information you gather be dated or untimely. All sources have to be cited following Modern Language Association (MLA) guidelines. Questions raised by your research should be explicit.

Using the Internet

Online sources that allow writers to get works published at little to no cost either as an e-book or a printed book are now widely available. There are editing as well as marketing services offered on many Internet sites. Writing tools offer help with everything from style to grammar. Sites for research are reliable, and offer accurate and objective information. Make sure you cite Internet sources using an accepted format such as that from the MLA (Modern Language Association). There are free online tools that can be accessed to allow people to work together on projects no matter how far apart they are geographically. Chat rooms and topic websites allow for an unprecedented exchange of information. Shared writing projects let you get adult input or brainstorm with your peers.

Gathering Relevant Information from Multiple Print and Digital Sources

Before compiling information from multiple print and digital sources, you must first decide how much information you need based on the scope of the project, and you must determine how knowledgeable your audience is. Make an outline of the similarities as well as the differences you encounter in various sources. Journals, text books, magazines, newspapers, and even texts written by other students: the number of sources you can uncover is limited only by your imagination. Strike a balance between being too detailed and bogged down, and too general and oversimplified. Whatever the source, verify how timely, accurate, and credible it is. You can avoid plagiarism, or using another person's words without acknowledgement, by following MLA (Modern Language Association) guidelines when you cite their works.

F. *Scott Fitzgerald's novel The Great Gatsby takes place on Long Island (near New York City) in the 1920s, during an era known as the Jazz Age. Discuss what the author's subject reveals about American society at that time.*

Fitzgerald was writing about a time when there was a period of great wealth in the country, as well as great excess and abandon, after the end of World War I. He portrays society's fascination with the ideals of wealth and happiness, the so-called "American Dream." The two main characters, Nick and Gatsby, both of whom served their country during the war, are cynical and disillusioned. Gatsby throws lavish parties at his estate every weekend with liquor (outlawed by the Eighteenth Amendment) flowing freely. Fitzgerald captures the mood with striking clarity, portraying the moral emptiness of the time and the growing distrust of the wealthy as the decade careened towards its close with the Great Depression of 1929.

Evaluate the Purpose of the Following Excerpt from Franklin D. Roosevelt's Speech of July 2, 1932.

> "I pledge you, I pledge myself, to a new deal for the American people. Let us all here assembled constitute ourselves prophets of a new order of competence and of courage. This is more than a political campaign; it is a call to arms..."

In this speech given by Franklin D. Roosevelt when he accepted the Democratic nomination for President, he proposed launching a new effort to turn back the tide of Depression that had gripped the country for several years. In using the phrase "a call to arms," he addressed the audience in a manner similar to how a commander would address his soldiers. His purpose was to contrast himself and the Democratic Party with the Republican view of government, which favored big businesses and a continuation of the policies of Herbert Hoover. He subsequently went on to win in a landslide victory in November, and his policies, of course, went on to be labeled by history as The New Deal.

MAKE WRITING A HABIT

In today's information driven society, writing is a skill that is of utmost importance in adult life. Writing, whether it is a short paragraph or two or an extended thesis, should come easily and smoothly (and should even be second nature) for those who wish to be successful. As such, writing should become a habit. An adult who follows the old adage "the more you write, the better you write" is sure to achieve recognition in any field of endeavor. It is important to study the writing process—the conscious effort of note taking, writing drafts, editing, and revising—so that you will grasp the concept of fine tuning your writing to different audiences, and will feel equally at ease writing a short note or a thoroughly researched treatise.

Persuasive text

INTRODUCING AN ARGUMENT IN A PERSUASIVE PASSAGE

The best way to introduce an argument in a persuasive passage and to structure it is to begin by organizing your thoughts and researching the evidence carefully. You should write everything down in outline format to start. Make sure you put the claim at the beginning of the passage. Then, list the reasons and the evidence that you have to support the claim. It is important that you provide enough evidence. Reasons and evidence should follow each other in a logical order. Write the passage so that you hold the reader's attention; use a strong tone and choose words carefully for maximum effect. If you can get the reader to understand your claim, he or she will be more likely to agree with your argument. Restate your claim in the concluding paragraph to maximize the impact on the reader.

MAKING A CLAIM

When making a claim, it is important to first think about the arguments that support that claim. While researching, try to anticipate what readers might say; this will help you thoroughly develop your claim. It is not enough to research a claim on the Internet, because many sources are dubious at best. Look for sites that are objective. Find authorities that you can quote, and use statistics. Present counterclaims using ample evidence. Mention both the strengths and weaknesses without any prejudice. Divide each counterclaim into a separate paragraph with supporting evidence. Make sure to present everything in a logical manner so that the information will be easily understood by the reader. Most importantly, one needs to separate opinions from facts.

CREATING COHESION

The best way to create cohesion between claims and evidence is to organize your ideas, and then write sentences explaining your reasons and evidence that logically follow your main ideas. Careful research will result in your argument being cohesive and easy to understand. Your claim and evidence must be clearly related to each other. Sometimes, it is useful to include metaphors, similes, or analogies to make your point clearer. Words and phrases that will indicate to the reader that the claim and evidence are related include "since," "because," "as a consequence," and "as a result." You can also utilize clauses to demonstrate a relationship between the reason and the effect. This approach is illustrated in the following sentence: "Since the sun now rose earlier in the morning, the birds awakened earlier and began their song." The first clause sets the tone, and it establishes causality between the reason and the effect. After writing, reread your text to verify that the relationships between cause and effect are logical.

FORMAL STYLE

A formal style is important when you want your writing to be objective and precise. A few requirements must be met to achieve this. It is important not to use fragments; write in complete sentences. Avoid contractions, and do not change tenses between sentences or paragraphs. Do not use the words "I" or "you"; this will add a more serious tone to your writing. Whenever possible, avoid using the passive tense. Using the active voice will make your writing more focused and interesting. Ensure your spelling is correct and that you follow all punctuation rules. Finally, make sure your ideas are presented in a logical order.

READ THE FOLLOWING PASSAGE AND SUGGEST SOME WAYS TO MAKE IT MORE FORMAL.

> When I was a kid growing up, I remember I had a lot of hard times. As a teenager, other kids used to make fun of me and call me names. It was really depressing. I couldn't find anyone to take to the prom. Sometimes, it was hard to keep up with all my homework.

HERE IS ONE WAY TO REWRITE IT:

> Becoming a teenager can be a stressful time. Adolescence involves both physical and emotional changes. Peer pressure and pressure at school cause many teenagers to have anxiety disorders; some even suffer from mild to severe depression. Boys and girls both worry about their physical appearance and about being popular.

The account is presented in the third person to make the passage more authoritative and formal. Complex sentences are utilized to keep the writing varied and interesting. Personal emotions are expressed in a more objective manner. A higher level of vocabulary results in a more precise, informed, and impressive finished text.

CONCLUDING STATEMENT

A concluding statement is an important part of a persuasive passage because it sets the tone for the reader and adds a sense of completion. A concluding sentence should not just repeat what was already said; the concluding statement should tie everything together. The concluding sentence should basically restate the importance of the argument. By doing this in the concluding paragraph, the impact on the reader will be maximized, and you will be more likely to bring the reader over to your side of an argument. The conclusion should logically fit into the flow of your passage. A good concluding statement serves to cement the bonds you have developed with the reader, and provides one more opportunity to get the reader on your side.

WHAT KIND OF ARGUMENT WOULD THE FOLLOWING CONCLUDING SENTENCE BE BEST SUITED FOR?

> As a result, soccer is the most popular sport in the world.

The sentence makes a good concluding sentence for a passage about the reasons why soccer (called football outside of the US) is the most popular sport in the world. Arguments can include the fact that players do not need any special equipment, while players of a similar sport—American football—need equipment such as helmets and protective padding. Another good angle is the fact that players don't have to be a certain size to play soccer, whereas the sport of American football places a premium on very large players, especially when filling defensive positions. Basketball, another sport that is also popular, requires a wooden court and two metal baskets with nets installed at a certain height. The concluding sentence provided would tie all the elements of the argument together.

Informational or Explanatory Text

INTRODUCING A TOPIC

An informational or explanatory text should have an introduction to the topic that the text will cover. One way you can accomplish this is by using a topic sentence, with details that support your thesis included afterwards. Another tactic is to use a reference to something going on in the modern world, even if your topic relates to something in the past. This makes your topic immediately more relevant. Some writers like to preview the ideas and concepts they are going to discuss by showing their relevance to a main topic. You could also preview concepts by demonstrating how they relate to everyday life.

Developing a Topic

It is important to develop the topic of an informational or explanatory text by utilizing relevant facts that clearly support the main topic. Include a topic sentence followed by any supporting details. These details should preferably be concrete facts that you have carefully researched, and which you are certain are accurate. You can also provide quotes taken from known experts in a field that is relevant to your topic. Quotes not only lend credibility to your thesis, but can also make your writing more varied and interesting. Diverse multimedia techniques, charts, and examples will also enhance your presentation. However, you should make sure these techniques play a supportive role, and are not presented solely to make your text look flashy.

Creating Cohesion

Experienced writers know how to use appropriate transitions to create cohesion in a text. They serve to clarify the relationships between ideas and concepts. Transition words or phrases such as "consequently," "therefore," and "as a result of" indicate causality between ideas. "However," "on the other hand," "in contrast," "but," and "similarly" indicate a compare and contrast relationship. You can also draw attention to examples by using words and phrases like "namely," "for example," "for instance," and "that is." When you need to show the order of importance of ideas or concepts, use transitions such as "at first," "primarily," "secondly," "former," or "latter."

Using Precise Language and Domain-Specific Vocabulary

Writers of informational or explanatory texts must use precise language and domain specific vocabulary in order to accurately get their ideas across. General vocabulary words will not bring home the points you are trying to make. Your audience will not follow your thesis closely if the text lacks the details that are supplied by carefully chosen, precise, and domain specific language. Using the word "isobar" in a text about meteorology, for instance, would be more effective than using the word "pressure." During the research stage, make sure you closely study the vocabulary used. Use a dictionary to clarify the meanings of words and terms you do not understand.

Establishing and Maintaining a Formal Style

Experienced writers use a formal style when they are writing explanatory or informational texts to lend greater credence to their material. They do not use an informal or colloquial tone, and they utilize the third person for objectivity. They use complex sentences, which are longer and add a further tone of formality and depth to the subject. By using a formal style, they show that they are serious about their subject. They are striving to make supporting details clear and to the point, but they are also presenting them in as much complexity as the intended audience can absorb. There is no introduction of personal opinion, unless that opinion can be carefully justified.

Importance of a Good Concluding Statement

A good concluding statement should sum up the overall intention of the text, and serves to "wrap up" the passage so that the reader is aware that you arrived at the logical ending of your argument. The conclusion should review the most salient points that you made, the reasoning you employed, and the supporting arguments for your reasoning. It serves to reinforce in the reader's mind that you did not leave anything out. The reader should not feel that there is more pertinent information that may follow. A good conclusion allows the reader to sit back and weigh the overall impact of your thesis, and it greatly increases the effectiveness of a text.

Narratives

SETTING THE STAGE

To set the stage for a narrative, you need to introduce the reader to the setting and the characters. Next, you should introduce a plot line. This should consist of various events that lead to a problem, a climax, and a resolution. This gives a narrative structure. The way in which the author introduces these elements has an influence on the overall effectiveness of the narrative. Make sure to use language to describe the setting and the characters that will grab the reader's attention. Make the details specific. The conclusion or resolution will allow you to tie up the details of the story.

INTRODUCING A NARRATOR

The narrator in a story is the person doing the "speaking," or the one who is telling the story. A narrator can speak in the first or third person. The narrator can shift from one person to another during the course of the story. It is even possible for the narrator to be non-human. The introduction of your narrator can be quick, subtle, dramatic, or humorous; it is up to you. Many times, an event or a circumstance opens the story. Make sure any details about time, place, and circumstance are developed logically and naturally, and that the reader will understand who (or what) the narrator is and where the narrator fits into the story.

USING TECHNIQUES

Writers employ numerous techniques to bring a narrative to life. Dialogue is one tool; it gives the reader a sense of what is happening, and also adds color and nuance to characters or the narrator. What a character says and how he says it portrays how that character feels. Pacing is also used in a narrative. The rhythms of the sentences, whether they are short or long, allow a writer to use time to the best effect, and to add color and depth to the events in the narrative. The plot line or sequence of events in the narrative is the actual structure of the story, and is developed from the opening of the story through one or more actions. These actions eventually lead to a climax, and then a resolution. The use of descriptions lets the reader visualize what is happening.

INTERJECTING SEQUENCE

Sequence should come in an order that can be easily grasped by the reader. It is a function of a natural flow of events, dialogue, and plot. Sequence should enhance what is happening in the story, and it should never seem forced or unnatural. A pattern should emerge, and it must make sense to the reader. Often times, a writer will make use of a flashback, a literary device where the writer goes back in time, and where events do not follow in sequence. When crafted properly, the flashback will make sense in the context of the story. Flashbacks can often add a sense of mystery or suspense to a narrative. Chronological narration, which puts events in the order in which they happened, is another literary device, and is used more frequently than flashbacks.

USING PRECISE LANGUAGE

Precise language is important in a narrative. It helps ensure that the concepts you are trying to communicate are readily understood by the audience. Precise language will be livelier, and will provoke more thought on the part of the reader. It includes the proper use of dialogue and imagery to get the point of the story across as succinctly as possible, so that there is nothing vague in the narrative. Your use of language should show an articulate grasp and control of the plot, and the whole text should be cohesive. Sensory language (which brings up images of the senses) can add extra detail and feeling, and can be very persuasive. Understanding the full range of language will result in a better narrative.

Importance of the Conclusion

The conclusion to a narrative is extremely important. An inadequate or poorly thought out conclusion can leave the reader confused and unable to tie everything together, or "wrap things up." There must be some type of resolution to whatever was described in the opening and the events that followed. A conclusion is not repetition; it is resolution. The resolution can be a summary. It could be a quotation. The resolution does not have to be clear cut. In fact, it may leave a lot unanswered. It could end with a rhetorical question or questions. Indeed, unlike traditional writing, conclusions in modern literature often present more questions than answers. In every case, however, the conclusion will leave the reader with no doubt that the narrative is over.

Doreen is writing a short story about training her dog Lola to compete in an agility competition. She has written about all that she has done to train her dog over the past three months. She is preparing to write a conclusion to her story. Describe what Doreen should try to accomplish with her conclusion.

Doreen should write a conclusion to tie everything together. Since she was training her dog Lola to compete, the end of the story should tell whether Lola won the competition. Doreen should describe the day of the competition and the result. This is the most obvious conclusion for her story. Doreen should bring her story to a close with a fitting and appropriate ending so that the reader will know exactly what the outcome was, and will not be left hanging in the end. The opening and all the events that happened lead up to this, and there is a form to her story.

Speaking and Listening

Discussions

Preparing for a Discussion on a Particular Topic

It is exceedingly important to prepare for class discussions. These discussions are important because they help prepare students for future discussions, and also allow them to practice effective techniques and learn communication skills. The exchanging of ideas is a skill that will remain with a student throughout his or her lifetime. When preparing for such a discussion, a student should research the subject at hand using the Internet and other sources. They should make sure they have read all essential applicable information. It is also important to have the resources (quotes, statistics, and audio visual material) you will need during the discussion on hand. A useful technique is to rehearse your role; practice the day before with a family member or a friend. Determine what you are going to focus on. If you are leading the discussion, think ahead about how you are going to guide the discussion to a conclusion, and how much time will be needed.

Rules for Collegial Discussions

Properly organized collegial discussions can be very productive, and can result in many new and interesting ideas being formulated and brought out in the classroom. It is important that rules be set up to promote civil, democratic discussions. Guidelines for the discussion should be established, which should include how much time each participant will be allowed to talk and then respond. There should be clear roles. Specific goals need to be established, and the progress towards reaching those goals should be tracked, with a deadline for completion kept in mind. Participants should learn how to use questions to add detail and depth to the discussion, and how to build on and further ideas that are put forth by others. It is important to try to understand and communicate with individuals who have a different perspective, especially from a cultural point of view. Everyone should be able to make use of evidence, and should be able to express themselves clearly within the structured framework.

Ways to Pose Questions That Elicit Elaboration

Asking questions that will encourage a response from others and propel a conversation entails asking specific, not general, questions, since they force the listener to think. Ideally, questions should be open-ended (i.e. they can't be answered with a simple "yes" or "no"). It is important to be proficient at asking questions, and at learning the art of asking the right question. Being a good listener is key to asking good questions. You should build on the ideas expressed by others in the classroom. One technique is asking a question at the end of what you have to say. You could ask something like, "Does that answer your question?" This helps personalize questions. Another overlooked technique is to take notes. It is also important to prevent people from straying from the subject by taking control of the situation and diplomatically steering the conversation back to the subject at hand.

Ensuring That a Full Range of Positions Are Equally Covered

Guidelines for the discussion should stress allowing each member of the team to express his or her viewpoint without prejudice. Each member should receive the same amount of time to put forth a theory or thesis, or to address a subject through an analytical probe without interruption. On the other hand, every team member should also be granted time to respond to individual presentations. Emotional outbursts do not have a place in this kind of discussion, nor do personal comments that pull away from an objective and intelligent discussion. When there is a divergence of opinion, the greatest of respect should be given to the opposing viewpoints.

RESPOND TO DIVERSE PERSPECTIVES

Key to responding to diverse perspectives is listening and keeping an open mind. Divergent ideas could be compiled by the entire discussion group in a list. Then, the link between the ideas could be identified, and it might be determined through consensus which opinions require more scrutiny or research. A goal should be set for the investigation or task, and assignments made so that any further research that is needed is done. The conversation can then resume with this new additional information kept in mind. This process is an orderly means of reaching a deeper understanding of a topic that not everyone may agree with or about.

INTEGRATING VARIOUS SOURCES OF INFORMATION THAT ARE PRESENTED IN DIVERSE FORMATS AND MEDIA

There are many different sources of information. On the Internet, there are multiple sites (some more reliable than others) where print information as well as charts and other graphic organizers are available to all. In addition, there are hard copy and online journals, textbooks, magazines, and newspapers; researchers are often overwhelmed with information. It is best to choose only the sources that can be verified or are from a credible author or organization. This information must then be analyzed to see how consistent it is and whether valid discrepancies exist, and why. After, it can be used in a presentation or a discussion.

ANALYZING A SPEAKER'S POINT OF VIEW

The point of view of a speaker needs to be determined to evaluate whether there is a clear delineation between evidence and the speaker's theory. If a speaker's viewpoint is prejudiced or based on emotion, this needs to be identified by evaluating the evidence. It is important to evaluate a speaker's choice of words and tone to determine whether the speech is tinged with feeling or objective. The evidence that a speaker uses to back up claims must also be closely evaluated to determine its source and validity. Many speakers are able to influence an audience through their strength of delivery, but if studied, there may be holes in logic or faults in the evidence that is used to prove a point.

PRESENTING CLAIMS, FINDINGS, AND SUPPORTING EVIDENCE

When in a focused discussion, be prepared to present your claims, findings, and supporting evidence in a clear and distinct manner. This means being prepared. When compiling your data, make sure to create an outline that has the main ideas and then the supporting evidence, including graphics that you want to present. Attention to details will result in a successful presentation, one in which the diverse individuals in the group will come away with a feeling of having been part of something meaningful. Facts and examples should be stressed. Repetition creates retention. It is important for the speaker to choose the right words, and to build momentum by gradually building up to the strongest argument(s). Graphics are important, because participants will be more convinced if they can see evidence as well as hear it. By breaking up the flow of the discussion and introducing pauses before and after pertinent arguments, the speaker will make the presentation of facts more interesting.

Presentations

One way to bring a presentation to life is to use digital media, including graphics, audio, visual, and interactive elements. Such tools will not only make a presentation more interesting and memorable, but will also keep those listening from distancing themselves from the presentation. It is easy for audience members to become bored during a presentation if they don't feel included. Digital media can effectively hold their interest. Graphics, diagrams, charts, and maps all serve to reinforce the point you are trying to make. The simpler these forms of media are, the more effective they will be. They serve to help the audience understand your argument; a video or audio can enhance the claims and findings of a presentation. Both visuals and multimedia components should be considered aids; they are not going to do the work for you. It is useful to rehearse the presentation until it flows smoothly.

When giving a speech, you need to make sure you feel confident in front of your audience. Exchange nerves for a funny story to open; have a variety of multimedia graphics that will pull your audience in. Perhaps most important, use the English language correctly when you speak. This is a situation where using correct grammar is essential. Before you speak, write your speech out and make sure that it demonstrates a command of correct conventions. In addition, be sure to speak clearly and slowly, and to enunciate words. Make sure the words that you choose have the correct literal meaning and the intended connotations. Try to avoid hesitations that end with "uh" or "er," which only distract from what you are saying. Look at one person in the audience and talk to her or him. Maintaining a smile will help create an atmosphere of informality. Extra effort needs to be made to avoid being wordy. Redundancy is sure to make audience attention wander.

Eye contact is one of the most important tactics for an effective presentation. When you maintain eye contact with audience members, you can be assured that your listeners will find your presentation believable. They will also be more likely to remember what you said. Reading a speech instead of giving one will have little impact on your audience. Make sure to look people in the eyes and smile. Use a voice that can be easily heard, and enunciate words so people will not be left wondering what was said. Remember to adapt your voice to the task at hand. Are you trying to persuade, look for sympathy, or tell an amazing story? All of these scenarios should yield a different voice and way of presenting the material. Most important of all, relax!

Language

USAGE IS A MATTER OF CONVENTION

Latin is an ancient language. It does not change. But English, like any modern language, may change over time. New words are always being introduced into the English language. Words are adapted from other languages. Examples of adapted words are taco, pizza, and karaoke. Usage, which is a matter of convention, can also change and evolve over time. It is not always clear what the correct form is, since there are sometimes two possibilities. For instance, the use of the subjunctive is much less prevalent today than it was in the past. The answer to the question of whether it is acceptable to begin a question with the word "and" or "but" has also changed. Years ago, this was strictly against usage rules, but it is now common practice in less formal texts.

USE OF THE SERIAL COMMA

The rules regarding use of the serial comma differ depending on whether a text is academic or more informal. Traditionally, and in academia, a comma is always used before the "and" in a list of items. This is not the case in more casual texts, such as newspapers, where the convention is not to use a comma before the word "and" in a list of items. This is just one example of how usage conventions are not always rigid, and can change according to the usage of the moment. A general rule of thumb is that a comma should be used in front of the "and" in a list of items if the text is for a school-related or academic use, but should not be used if the text is intended for everyday use.

MARINA AND KEEGAN ARE WRITING A REPORT TOGETHER. THEY ARE HAVING A DISAGREEMENT ABOUT WHETHER A SPLIT INFINITIVE MARINA USED IN ONE SENTENCE IS GRAMMATICALLY CORRECT. MARINA THINKS THE SPLIT INFINITIVE IS FINE IN THIS INSTANCE, BUT KEEGAN DOES NOT AGREE. HOW CAN THEY COME TO A RESOLUTION ABOUT THIS ISSUE?

There are many grey areas related to English usage, and split infinitives is one of them. The strict notion that they should never be used is less in vogue today than it was a few years ago, and they may now even be found in formal writing. However, if the text that is being prepared is academic, it is probably best to avoid using them. In English, it is always possible to word things differently to avoid awkward usage, and this is also true for split infinitives. Marina and Keegan could consult *Merriam-Webster's Dictionary of English Usage* or *Garner's Modern American Usage* to figure out what they should do. Typically, however, the more academic the paper, the more formal the usage should be.

RULES OF HYPHENATION

Hyphens are used in many instances. They are used to join compound words, whether nouns or verbs. The best way to determine if a word needs a hyphen is to check it in the dictionary. They are used to separate two or more adjectives when they come before a noun. They are used to hyphenate all compound numbers from *twenty-one* through *ninety-nine*. They are used to hyphenate all spelled-out fractions. They are used to hyphenate prefixes when they come before proper nouns. They are used to hyphenate all words beginning with *self* except *selfish* and *selfless*. They are used in some titles, such as vice-president. It is important not to confuse a hyphen with a dash.

CORRECT THE PUNCTUATION IN THE FOLLOWING SENTENCE.

> The forty year old man jumped over the bramble covered fence rail, where he came upon a too good to be true treasure chest filled with gold pieces that were really chocolate candies.

THE CORRECT WAY TO WRITE THIS SENTENCE IS: THE FORTY-YEAR-OLD MAN JUMPED OVER THE BRAMBLE-COVERED FENCE RAIL, WHERE HE CAME UPON A TOO-GOOD-TO-BE-TRUE TREASURE CHEST FILLED WITH GOLD PIECES THAT WERE REALLY CHOCOLATE CANDIES.

Hyphens are used to join several adjectives modifying a noun when they cannot be joined by the word "and." "Forty," "year," and "old" all modify man and are hyphenated; these modifiers cannot be joined by "and." The same is true of "bramble covered." It would be awkward to say bramble and covered. The two words work together to create a description, so they are hyphenated. The last group of adjectives is "too," "good," and "to be true," which is really an expression that needs to be hyphenated. It is important not to confuse a hyphen with a dash; a dash is used to punctuate clauses, not adjectives. Although not shown here, hyphens are also used to punctuate titles such as "vice-president."

COMMON SPELLING ERRORS

CORRECT THE SPELLING IN THE SENTENCE BELOW.

> The visitors will aclimate to the enviromment as soon as they become accustomed to the surroundings of the tropacs.

The words that are misspelled are "aclimate," which should be "acclimate"; "environmment," which is spelled "environment"; and "tropacs," which is spelled "tropics." It is important to learn to spell words correctly. One way to learn how to spell words is to learn how to sound out words. Break longer words down into syllables, and into affixes and roots. Get the correct spelling from a dictionary, and then practice that spelling. Practice with a few words at a time; use them in sentences. Then move on to new vocabulary words. It is also useful to remember spelling rules, such as "i before e except after c" (receive), "drop the final e" (like, liking), and "double the last consonant" when adding suffixes (stop, stopped).

SYNTAX

Syntax is the order of the words in a sentence. When writing, it is important to make sure not only that the syntax is correct, but also that it is not repetitive. There is nothing worse than reading a passage that has sentences that are all alike: noun, verb, object. These need to be interspersed with sentences that use a variety of clause constructions. This will lend a musicality to the writing, and will allow for greater flow of language and ideas. Make sure to reread any written material to ensure that the syntax is correct and engaging. Otherwise, you may end up with something that comes off as confused rather than well-written.

REWRITE THE FOLLOWING SENTENCES BY VARYING THEIR SYNTAX.

> Marilyn and Rosemary worked together. They were having a party. They had to get all the food done first. They cleaned the house and decorated. They invited about 20 people. The people were all work associates. They were having the party in Marilyn's backyard. This is where she had many similar parties. They were always fun.

THIS IS ONE WAY TO REWRITE THE SENTENCES SO THAT THE SYNTAX IS VARIED:

Marilyn and Rosemary, who worked together, were going to have a party. But before they could do that, they had to get all the food ready for it, as well as clean the house and decorate. They invited about 20 people, who were all work associates, and were holding the party in Marilyn's backyard, where there had been many other parties that were always fun.

The rewritten sentences provide a greater variety of syntax, and consequently, greater rhythm. The language is more engaging as a result. Remember to make use of clauses to introduce information and create sentences that are complex. In addition, remember to reread any work you rewrite to make sure it makes sense.

Context Clues

The term "context clues" refers to the words or phrases in the sentences that surround a new word or phrase. Context clues can often allow the reader to figure out the meaning of an unfamiliar word or phrase. Context clues may include examples of the new word or phrase, synonyms, antonyms, definitions, or contrasting information. By using context clues in the surrounding sentences, the reader can figure out approximately what the unknown word or phrase means. The placement of a word or a phrase is important, as is its function in a sentence. If a word or a phrase is being used as an adjective, the reader should look at the other adjectives in the sentence or the surrounding sentences to see if there is a clue to the word's or phrase's meaning. The location of a word or a phrase is also important. For instance, if a word or a phrase is at the beginning of a sentence, try to figure out its consequence; this may help the reader figure out its meaning.

Using context clues, determine the meaning of "fortuitous" as it is used in the following excerpt.

> Warren felt that meeting his nephew was quite fortuitous, since his nephew showed a real interest in getting involved in the company's business. Warren was hopeful that someday his nephew could take over for him.

To figure out the meaning of the word "fortuitous," the reader needs to analyze the rest of the sentence, as well as the following sentence. It would appear that their meeting was a good thing, since Warren was hopeful that his nephew could take over for him. The adjective "hopeful" helps the reader come to the conclusion that "fortuitous" means good or lucky. This is just one of the context clues. Another one would be that the nephew showed a real interest in his uncle's business. Always make sure to study the surrounding phrases and sentences for clues to an unknown word. The placement of the word or phrase and its function in the sentence are also important.

Explain how context clues can help the reader figure out the meaning of the phrase "prosthetic device" in the following excerpt.

> Modern artificial limbs are much better than artificial limbs of the past. These prosthetic devices have made it possible for amputees to run and to compete in sports. For instance, Vietnam veteran Bill Demby is able to play basketball in an aggressive, fast-paced, competitive manner thanks to high-tech plastic legs.

The placement of the phrase "prosthetic devices" helps the reader understand that the phrase is another way of saying "modern artificial limbs." This is the subject of the excerpt; the term "prosthetic devices" is a synonym for "modern artificial limbs." Even if the reader does not understand the meaning of "prosthetic," he or she can figure out the meaning of the expression. This shows how placement and context clues can assist a reader in learning the meaning of a word or an expression. Always study the information in an excerpt to better understand what is being said. The conclusion of the second sentence reinforces the meaning of the phrase by providing another synonym: "high-tech plastic legs."

How Certain Endings Can Indicate What Part of Speech a Word Is

The suffix of a word can be extremely important in telling a reader what function the word has in a sentence. Certain endings are used to make a stem an adjective; others are used to make a stem a noun. For instance, the root *consider* has many forms. It becomes a noun—*consideration*—with the addition of *-ation*. It becomes an adjective—*considerate*—with the addition of the suffix *-ate*. The adverb *considerately* can be made from the adjective *considerate* by adding *-ly*. This is a simple yet sophisticated method of figuring out what part of speech a word is.

The root word for *absolution* is *absolute*. The suffix *-tion* indicates that the word is a noun. The root could be combined with other suffixes to make other parts of speech as well. Add an *–ly* and you have the adverb *absolutely*. This word is a noun in its root form (*absolute*), so no change is needed to it. To make the verb *absolve*, the suffix *–ve* is added. This word is irregular, since most roots tend to be in verb form. It is important to be able to analyze a word, not just for its etymology, but also to determine what part of speech the word might be.

Discuss the etymology of the word fluctuate in the following sentence.

Tommy's mother noticed that his emotions tended to *fluctuate* a lot.

There really isn't a context clue in this statement, so you need to look up the word and discover its etymology to learn more about its meaning. The dictionary says that *fluctuate* is an intransitive verb, meaning it has no object. There are three syllables: fluc.tu.ate. The word has a Latin origin. It is derived from the verb "fluctuare," which means to undulate. You will also need to look up the word "undulate." It means to move in a wave-like motion, or to change continually. Synonyms of *fluctuate* are "alter," "shift," "swing," and "hesitate." In this usage, you can also see that there is a connotation of unpredictability. These clues give you a better understanding of the statement.

Using Specialized Reference Materials to Determine the Pronunciation of a Word

A print or digital dictionary can be used to find out many things about a word. A dictionary will show the correct pronunciation of a word, provide its meaning, and identify what part of speech the word is. It will also tell how the word was derived—that is, what words it came from originally. A dictionary will have a guide that shows how to sound out the words; it will use symbols to indicate sounds, and will also use sample sounds (the "a" in "bad," for instance). A dictionary lists all of the meanings of a word and the parts of speech the word can be used as. A thesaurus is useful because it lists synonyms for all the various meanings of a word, and it can help you clarify the precise meaning of a word as it is used in the text you are reading. This means you can find other words to use in a report or a text that mean the same thing as a word that may be used too often. Many books will have a glossary at the end to help you understand difficult or unfamiliar words used in the text.

Read the sentence below. Determine the meaning of "a partisan response."

While at the meeting of the homeowners' association, Jeannie had the distinct feeling that there was a partisan response when all the other tenants belligerently shouted that they were just not going to accept any more increases in maintenance assessments, no matter what the condition of the roof was.

The meaning of the phrase can be determined from the context clues in the sentence. One big clue is the fact that the "other tenants belligerently shouted..." This suggests a tone of prejudice or unreasonableness. The sentence further suggests that there was something wrong with the roof that needed repairing, and that "no matter what," the other tenants were not willing to pay. Therefore, the reader can come to the conclusion that the phrase refers to a prejudiced reaction or response. If there were not enough clues in the sentence to determine the phrase's meaning, the word "partisan" could be looked up in a dictionary. Its meaning would explain the meaning of the phrase.

Analyze the following statement by Jesus Christ, which is found in the New Testament of the Bible.

"If anyone comes to me and does not hate his own father and mother and wife and children and brothers and sisters, yes, and even his own life, he cannot be my disciple. And whoever does not carry their cross and follow me cannot be my disciple."(Luke 14:25-27)

This statement by Jesus that is quoted by Luke is an example of hyperbole. Hyperbole, or exaggeration to make a point, is frequently used throughout the Bible. It is not meant to be taken literally, and there is no command to hate family members or oneself. Rather, it is an entreaty that is meant to arouse intense emotion for maximum effect. The next sentence offers a clue in context for the reader's interpretation: one must be able to carry one's own cross (work hard) to be a disciple of Christ (i.e. to be a devout Christian). Therefore, the meaning is that devotion to God is more important than any relationship to any other family member, or any self-interest.

Nuances of "Superfluous" and "Outmoded"

Nuances are slight differences in the meanings of words that mean nearly the same thing. Nuances give words different tones or shades of meaning. They are similar to connotations, although usually more subtle. In the case of the words "superfluous" and "outmoded," superfluous conveys the sense that something is not and probably was never needed, while outmoded simply suggests that something is no longer of value since it is rendered needless due to age. Writers often use nuance to suggest something rather than saying it directly. This is often done through the choice of word or words that are used. Readers should always be aware of nuances, and should take them into account when considering the overall intent of a text.

Comprehension

It is important to acquire and accurately use words and phrases at the appropriate level to improve comprehension of various school subjects. Comprehension of academic and domain specific words is crucial to understanding the ideas and theories you will encounter as you move further in your academic career or enter the work force. Increased word knowledge that is domain specific helps individuals attain their academic and career goals. Therefore, it is very important to develop a system for increasing vocabulary through reading, using word lists, understanding word etymologies, and using new words in academic or work-related settings. A good vocabulary will result in greater personal achievements at a variety of levels.

Practice Test #1

Practice Questions

Questions 1-5 pertain to the following excerpt.

Excerpt from Emma

by Jane Austen

Emma Woodhouse, handsome, clever, and rich, with a comfortable home and happy disposition, seemed to unite some of the best blessings of existence; and had lived nearly twenty-one years in the world with very little to distress or <u>vex</u> her.

She was the youngest of the two daughters of a most affectionate, indulgent father; and had, in consequence of her sister's marriage, been mistress of his house from a very early period. Her mother had died too long ago for her to have more than an indistinct remembrance of her caresses; and her place had been supplied by an excellent woman as governess, who had fallen little short of a mother in affection.

Sixteen years had Miss Taylor been in Mr. Woodhouse's family, less as a governess than a friend, very fond of both daughters, but particularly of Emma. Between them it was more the intimacy of sisters. Even before Miss Taylor had ceased to hold the nominal office of governess, the mildness of her temper had hardly allowed her to impose any restraint; and the shadow of authority being now long passed away, they had been living together as friend and friend very mutually attached, and Emma doing just what she liked; highly esteeming Miss Taylor's judgment, but directed chiefly by her own.

The real evils, indeed, of Emma's situation were the power of having rather too much her own way, and a disposition to think a little too well of herself; these were the disadvantages which threatened her many enjoyments. The danger, however, was at present so unperceived, that they did not by any means rank as misfortunes with her.

Sorrow came—a gentle sorrow—but not at all in the shape of any disagreeable consciousness—Miss Taylor married. It was Miss Taylor's loss which first brought grief. It was on the wedding-day of this beloved friend that Emma first sat in mournful thought of any continuance. The wedding over, and the bride-people gone, her father and herself were left to dine together, with no prospect of a third to cheer a long evening. Her father composed himself to sleep after dinner, as usual, and she had then only to sit and think of what she had lost.

The event had every promise of happiness for her friend. Mr. Weston was a man of unexceptionable character, easy fortune, suitable age, and pleasant manners; and there was some satisfaction in considering with what self-denying, generous friendship she had always wished and promoted the match; but it was a black morning's work for her. The want of Miss Taylor would be felt every hour of every day. She recalled her past kindness—the kindness, the affection of sixteen years—how she had taught and how she had played with her from five years old—how she had devoted all her powers to attach and amuse her in health—and how nursed her through the various illnesses of childhood. A large debt of gratitude was owing here...the equal footing and perfect unreserve which had soon followed Isabella's marriage, on their being left to each other, was yet a dearer, tenderer recollection. She had been a friend and companion such as few possessed: intelligent, well-informed, useful, gentle, knowing all the ways of the family, interested in all its concerns, and peculiarly interested in herself, in every pleasure, every scheme of hers—one to whom she could speak every thought as it arose, and who had such an affection for her as could never find fault.

How was she to bear the change?—It was true that her friend was going only half a mile from them; but Emma was aware that great must be the difference between a Mrs. Weston, only half a mile from them, and a Miss Taylor in the house; and with all her advantages, natural and domestic, she was now in great danger of suffering from intellectual solitude. She dearly loved her father, but he was no companion for her. He could not meet her in conversation, rational or playful.

The evil of the actual disparity in their ages (and Mr. Woodhouse had not married early) was much increased by his constitution and habits; for having been a valetudinarian all his life, without activity of mind or body, he was a much older man in ways than in years; and though everywhere beloved for the friendliness of his heart and his amiable temper, his talents could not have recommended him at any time.

Her sister, though comparatively but little removed by matrimony, being settled in London, only sixteen miles off, was much beyond her daily reach; and many a long October and November evening must be struggled through at Hartfield, before Christmas brought the next visit from Isabella and her husband, and their little children, to fill the house, and give her pleasant society again.

1. How does Miss Taylor's marriage affect Emma?

a. Miss Taylor's marriage disrupts the comfort Emma had enjoyed all her life.
b. Emma is happy her friend is marrying a wonderful man.
c. Emma regards the change as a challenge and opportunity for intellectual growth.
d. Miss Taylor's marriage makes Emma think about getting married herself.

This question has two parts. Answer Part A, then answer Part B.

2. Part A: As used in the first paragraph, what does the word "vex" mean?

a. interest
b. little
c. support
d. displease

Part B: What word from the excerpt gives you the best hint to the answer in Part A?

a. distress
b. fulfill
c. existence
d. frustrate

3. Based on this excerpt, Emma can be described as

a. unfortunate.
b. devious.
c. selfish.
d. studious.

4. How do themes of class and maturity interact in this excerpt?

a. Emma's upper-class background gives her greater access to education, thereby making her more interested in intellectual stimulation than a less mature person might be.
b. The privilege that comes with an upper-class background can prevent a person from having the necessary skills for dealing with change in a mature way.
c. Emma's first twenty-one years were so happy because she enjoyed a privileged, upper-class lifestyle, and that happiness made her a more mature person.
d. Having people constantly take care of her has prevented Emma from developing feelings of kindness and love for others.

5. Why does the author describe Miss Taylor's wedding as a "black morning's work"?

a. Emma has to work to pretend she is happy about the wedding.
b. The day of Miss Taylor's wedding is a bad day for Emma.
c. Emma worked hard to organize the wedding.
d. The wedding party dresses in black.

Questions 6-10 pertain to the following excerpt.

Excerpt from The Federalist No. 1

By Alexander Hamilton

To the People of the State of New York:

AFTER an unequivocal experience of the inefficacy of the subsisting federal government, you are called upon to deliberate on a new Constitution for the United States of America. The subject speaks its own importance; comprehending in its consequences nothing less than the existence of the UNION, the safety and welfare of the parts of which it is composed, the fate of an empire in many respects the most interesting in the world. It has been frequently remarked that it seems to have been reserved to the people of this country, by their conduct and example, to decide the important question, whether societies of men are really capable or not of establishing good government from reflection and choice, or whether they are forever destined to depend for their political constitutions on accident and force. If there be any truth in the remark, the crisis at which we are arrived may with propriety be regarded as the era in which that decision is to be made; and a wrong election of the part we shall act may, in this view, deserve to be considered as the general misfortune of mankind.

This idea will add the inducements of philanthropy to those of patriotism, to heighten the solicitude which all considerate and good men must feel for the event. Happy will it be if our choice should be directed by a judicious estimate of our true interests, unperplexed and unbiased by considerations not connected with the public good. But this is a thing more ardently to be wished than seriously to be expected. The plan offered to our deliberations affects too many particular interests, innovates upon too many local institutions, not to involve in its discussion a variety of objects foreign to its merits, and of views, passions and prejudices little favorable to the discovery of truth.

Among the most formidable of the obstacles which the new Constitution will have to encounter may readily be distinguished the obvious interest of a certain class of men in every State to resist all changes which may hazard a diminution of the power, emolument, and consequence of the offices they hold under the State establishments; and the perverted ambition of another class of men, who will either hope to aggrandize themselves by the confusions of their country, or will flatter themselves with fairer prospects of elevation from the subdivision of the empire into several partial confederacies than from its union under one government.

It is not, however, my design to dwell upon observations of this nature. I am well aware that it would be disingenuous to resolve indiscriminately the opposition of any set of men (merely because their situations might subject them to suspicion) into interested or ambitious views. Candor will oblige us to admit that even such men may be actuated by upright intentions; and it cannot be doubted that much of the opposition which has made its appearance, or may hereafter make its appearance, will spring from sources, blameless at least, if not respectable—the honest errors of minds led astray by preconceived jealousies and fears. So numerous indeed and so powerful are the causes which serve to give a false bias to the judgment, that we, upon many occasions, see wise and good men on the wrong as well as on the right side of questions of the first magnitude to society. This circumstance, if duly attended to, would furnish a lesson of moderation to those who are ever so much persuaded of their being in the right in any controversy. And a further reason for caution, in this respect, might be drawn from the reflection that we are not always sure that those who advocate the truth are influenced by purer principles than their antagonists. Ambition, avarice, personal animosity, party opposition, and many other motives not more laudable than these, are apt to operate as well upon those who support as those who oppose the right side of a question. Were there not even these inducements to moderation, nothing could be more ill-judged than that intolerant spirit which has, at all times, characterized political parties. For in politics, as in religion, it is equally absurd to aim at making proselytes by fire and sword. Heresies in either can rarely be cured by persecution.

And yet, however just these sentiments will be allowed to be, we have already sufficient indications that it will happen in this as in all former cases of great national discussion. A torrent of angry and malignant passions will be let loose. To judge from the conduct of the opposite parties, we shall be led to conclude that they will mutually hope to evince the justness of their opinions, and to increase the number of their converts by the loudness of their declamations and the bitterness of their invectives. An enlightened zeal for the energy and efficiency of government will be stigmatized as the offspring of a temper fond of despotic power and hostile to the principles of liberty. An over-scrupulous jealousy of danger to the rights of the people, which is more commonly the fault of the head than of the heart, will be represented as mere pretense and artifice, the stale bait for popularity at the expense of the public good. It will be forgotten, on the one hand, that jealousy is the usual concomitant of love, and that the noble enthusiasm of liberty is apt to be infected with a spirit of narrow and illiberal distrust. On the other hand, it will be equally forgotten that the vigor of government is essential to the security of liberty; that, in the contemplation of a sound and well-informed judgment, their interest can never be separated; and that a dangerous ambition more often lurks behind the specious mask of zeal for the rights of the people than under the forbidden appearance of zeal for the firmness and efficiency of government. History will teach us that the former has been found a much more certain road to the introduction of despotism than the latter, and that of those men who have overturned the liberties of republics, the greatest number have begun their career by paying an obsequious court to the people; commencing demagogues, and ending tyrants.

6. How does the opening of this excerpt affect the writer's argument?

a. By criticizing the United States Constitution explicitly, he is challenging readers to look at old institutions in new ways that may have positive effects on the federal government.
b. By portraying the subsisting federal government as suffering from inefficacy, he is seeking to alienate overly patriotic readers.
c. By saying that it is up to "the people of this country" to establish a "good government," he is suggesting that he expects input from his fellow Americans regarding how to improve the United States Constitution.
d. By drawing attention to the "unequivocal" "inefficacy" of the subsisting federal government, Alexander Hamilton immediately explains why the federal government is in need of change.

7. What effect does the author's use of first-person point of view have on his argument?

a. It attempts to establish agreement between the reader and himself.
b. It establishes an informal tone that makes him seem friendlier and more approachable.
c. It forces the reader to feel responsibility for the federal government's problems.
d. It implies the reader also needs to suggest methods for improving the federal government.

8. Which of the following sentences from the excerpt exemplifies an attempt to sway the reader's opinion of the writer's opponents?

a. And yet, however just these sentiments will be allowed to be, we have already sufficient indications that it will happen in this as in all former cases of great national discussion.
b. For in politics, as in religion, it is equally absurd to aim at making proselytes by fire and sword.
c. To judge from the conduct of the opposite parties, we shall be led to conclude that they will mutually hope to evince the justness of their opinions, and to increase the number of their converts by the loudness of their declamations and the bitterness of their invectives.
d. This idea will add the inducements of philanthropy to those of patriotism, to heighten the solicitude which all considerate and good men must feel for the event.

9. Why does the writer follow paragraph 3 by stating, "It is not, however, my design to dwell upon observations of this nature"?

a. He regrets criticizing politicians currently holding office and wants the reader to focus on the less inflammatory details in his argument.
b. He wants to give the impression that the purpose of his argument is not merely to criticize politicians who are currently holding office.
c. He realizes he lacks the information to continue criticizing politicians currently holding office and cannot continue his argument.
d. He believes that criticizing politicians currently holding office is a weak way to present his argument and will stop doing so.

10. As used in the final sentence of the excerpt, what does the word "obsequious" mean?

a. submissive
b. free
c. revolutionary
d. dominant

Questions 11-15 pertain to the following excerpt.

Second Inaugural Address

By Abraham Lincoln

Fellow-Countrymen:

AT this second appearing to take the oath of the Presidential office there is less occasion for an extended address than there was at the first. Then a statement somewhat in detail of a course to be pursued seemed fitting and proper. Now, at the expiration of four years, during which public declarations have been constantly called forth on every point and phase of the great contest which still absorbs the attention and engrosses the energies of the nation, little that is new could be presented. The progress of our arms, upon which all else chiefly depends, is as well known to the public as to myself, and it is, I trust, reasonably satisfactory and encouraging to all. With high hope for the future, no prediction in regard to it is ventured.

On the occasion corresponding to this four years ago all thoughts were anxiously directed to an impending civil war. All dreaded it, all sought to avert it. While the inaugural address was being delivered from this place, devoted altogether to saving the Union without war, insurgent agents were in the city seeking to destroy it without war—seeking to dissolve the Union and divide effects by negotiation. Both parties deprecated war, but one of them would make war rather than let the nation survive, and the other would accept war rather than let it perish, and the war came.

One-eighth of the whole population were colored slaves, not distributed generally over the Union, but localized in the southern part of it. These slaves constituted a peculiar and powerful interest. All knew that this interest was somehow the cause of the war. To strengthen, perpetuate, and extend this interest was the object for which the insurgents would rend the Union even by war, while the Government claimed no right to do more than to restrict the territorial enlargement of it. Neither party expected for the war the magnitude or the duration which it has already attained. Neither anticipated that the cause of the conflict might cease with or even before the conflict itself should cease. Each looked for an easier triumph, and a result less fundamental and astounding. Both read the same Bible and pray to the same God, and each invokes His aid against the other. It may seem strange that any men should dare to ask a just God's assistance in wringing their bread from the sweat of other men's faces, but let us judge not, that we be not judged. The prayers of both could not be answered. That of neither has been answered fully. The Almighty has His own purposes. "Woe unto the world because of offenses; for it must needs be that offenses come, but woe to that man by whom the offense cometh." If we shall suppose that American slavery is one of those offenses which, in the providence of God, must needs come, but which, having continued through His appointed time, He now wills to remove, and that He gives to both North and South this terrible war as the woe due to those by whom the offense came, shall we discern therein any departure from those divine attributes which the believers in a living God always ascribe to Him? Fondly do we hope, fervently do we pray, that this mighty scourge of war may speedily pass away. Yet, if God wills that it continue until all the wealth piled by the bondsman's two hundred and fifty years of unrequited toil shall be sunk, and until every drop of blood drawn with the lash shall be paid by another drawn with the sword, as was said three thousand years ago, so still it must be said "the judgments of the Lord are true and righteous altogether."

With malice toward none, with charity for all, with firmness in the right as God gives us to see the right, let us strive on to finish the work we are in, to bind up the nation's wounds, to care for him who shall have borne the battle and for his widow and his orphan, to do all which may achieve and cherish a just and lasting peace among ourselves and with all nations.

11. Why does Lincoln discuss his first inaugural address in this passage?

a. To prove that the country could have gone in a different direction.
b. To illustrate how the country had changed since his first inauguration.
c. To show how much he improved the country during his first term.
d. To explain that the country was once a place of peace.

12. Which sentence from the address supports the idea that Lincoln believed the North and the South did not have equally justifiable reasons for taking part in the war?

a. All knew that this interest was somehow the cause of the war.
b. Neither anticipated that the cause of the conflict might cease with or even before the conflict, itself, should cease.
c. Both parties deprecated war, but one of them would make war rather than let the nation survive, and the other would accept war rather than let it perish, and the war came.
d. Each looked for an easier triumph, and a result less fundamental and astounding.

13. How does Lincoln unite the themes of war and religion in his second inaugural address?

a. He suggests that the war and its end are parts of God's plan.
b. He says that no man would ask God to help him win a war.
c. He insists that it is God's responsibility, not his own, to resolve the war.
d. He quotes from the Bible liberally in order to extend an address he knew was too short.

14. How might reading Lincoln's address online differ from hearing it in person?

a. Lincoln likely was angry while reading his address, and this anger is lost in its translation to online text.
b. Lincoln's original address was much longer than the version that later appeared online.
c. Lincoln was an impressive-looking man, and this characteristic could be conveyed online only if the web page includes a photograph of him.
d. Lincoln would have been able to use his voice to heighten the emotion in his address.

15. What is the purpose of the final paragraph of Lincoln's address?

a. It is a sober remembrance for all who died during the American Civil War.
b. It is a warning that America could face new conflicts with other nations.
c. It is an attempt to forge a new feeling of union and caring between the North and the South.
d. It is a plea to other nations to seek peaceful solutions to conflicts with the United States.

Questions 16 – 25 pertain to the following story:

Anna Karenina
By Leo Tolstoy

(1) The young Princess Kitty Shcherbatskaya was eighteen. It was the first winter that she had been out in the world. Her success in society had been greater than that of either of her elder sisters, and greater even than her mother had anticipated. To say nothing of the young men who danced at the Moscow balls being almost all in love with Kitty, two serious suitors had already this first winter made their appearance: Levin, and immediately after his departure, Count Vronsky.

(2) Levin's appearance at the beginning of the winter, his frequent visits, and evident love for Kitty, had led to the first serious conversations between Kitty's parents as to her future, and to disputes between them. The prince was on Levin's side; he said he wished for nothing better for Kitty. The princess for her part, going round the question in the manner peculiar to women, maintained that Kitty was too young, that Levin had done nothing to prove that he had serious intentions, that Kitty felt no great attraction to him, and other side issues; but she did not state the principal point, which was that she looked for a better match for her daughter, and that Levin was not to her liking, and she did not understand him. When Levin had abruptly departed, the princess was delighted, and said to her husband triumphantly: "You see I was right." When Vronsky appeared on the scene, she was still more delighted, confirmed in her opinion that Kitty was to make not simply a good, but a brilliant match.

(3) In the mother's eyes there could be no comparison between Vronsky and Levin. She disliked in Levin his strange and uncompromising opinions and his shyness in society, founded, as she supposed, on his pride and his queer sort of life, as she considered it, absorbed in cattle and peasants. She did not very much like it that he, who was in love with her daughter, had kept coming to the house for six weeks, as though he were waiting for something, inspecting, as though he were afraid he might be doing them too great an honor by making an offer, and did not realize that a man, who continually visits at a house where there is a young unmarried girl, is bound to make his intentions clear. And suddenly, without doing so, he disappeared. "It's as well he's not attractive enough for Kitty to have fallen in love with him," thought the mother.

(4) Vronsky satisfied all the mother's desires. Very wealthy, clever, of aristocratic family, on the highroad to a brilliant career in the army and at court, and a fascinating man. Nothing better could be wished for.

(5) Vronsky openly flirted with Kitty at balls, danced with her, and came continually to the house, consequently there could be no doubt of the seriousness of his intentions. But, in spite of that, the mother had spent the whole of that winter in a state of terrible anxiety and agitation.

(6) Princess Shcherbatskaya had herself been married thirty years ago, her aunt arranging the match. Her husband, about whom everything was well known before hand, had come, looked at his future bride, and been looked at. The match-making aunt had ascertained and communicated their mutual impression. That impression had been favorable. Afterwards, on a day fixed beforehand, the expected offer was made to her parents, and accepted. All had passed very simply and easily. So it seemed, at least, to the princess. But over her own daughters she had felt how far from simple and easy is the business, apparently so commonplace, of marrying off one's daughters. The panics that had been lived through, the thoughts that had been brooded over, the money that had been wasted, and the disputes with her husband over marrying the two elder girls, Darya and Natalia! Now, since the youngest had come out, she was going through the same terrors, the same doubts, and still

more violent quarrels with her husband than she had over the elder girls. The old prince, like all fathers indeed, was exceedingly punctilious on the score of the honor and reputation of his daughters. He was irrationally jealous over his daughters, especially over Kitty, who was his favorite. At every turn he had scenes with the princess for compromising her daughter. The princess had grown accustomed to this already with her other daughters, but now she felt that there was more ground for the prince's touchiness. She saw that of late years much was changed in the manners of society, that a mother's duties had become still more difficult. She saw that girls of Kitty's age formed some sort of clubs, went to some sort of lectures, mixed freely in men's society; drove about the streets alone, many of them did not curtsey, and, what was the most important thing, all the girls were firmly convinced that to choose their husbands was their own affair, and not their parents'. "Marriages aren't made nowadays as they used to be," was thought and said by all these young girls, and even by their elders. But how marriages were made now, the princess could not learn from any one. The French fashion—of the parents arranging their children's future—was not accepted; it was condemned. The English fashion of the complete independence of girls was also not accepted, and not possible in Russian society. The Russian fashion of match-making by the offices of intermediate persons was for some reason considered unseemly; it was ridiculed by everyone, and by the princess herself. But how girls were to be married, and how parents were to marry them, no one knew. Everyone with whom the princess had chanced to discuss the matter said the same thing: "Mercy on us, it's high time in our day to cast off all that old-fashioned business. It's the young people have to marry; and not their parents; and so we ought to leave the young people to arrange it as they choose." It was very easy for anyone to say that who had no daughters, but the princess realized that in the process of getting to know each other, her daughter might fall in love, and fall in love with someone who did not care to marry her or who was quite unfit to be her husband. And, however much it was instilled into the princess that in our times young people ought to arrange their lives for themselves, she was unable to believe it, just as she would have been unable to believe that, at any time whatever, the most suitable playthings for children five years old ought to be loaded pistols. And so the princess was more uneasy over Kitty than she had been over her elder sisters.

(7) Now she was afraid that Vronsky might confine himself to simply flirting with her daughter. She saw that her daughter was in love with him, but tried to comfort herself with the thought that he was an honorable man, and would not do this. But at the same time she knew how easy it is, with the freedom of manners of today, to turn a girl's head, and how lightly men generally regard such a crime. The week before, Kitty had told her mother of a conversation she had with Vronsky during a mazurka. This conversation had partly reassured the princess; but perfectly at ease she could not be. Vronsky had told Kitty that both he and his brother were so used to obeying their mother that they never made up their minds to any important undertaking without consulting her. "And just now, I am impatiently awaiting my mother's arrival from Petersburg, as peculiarly fortunate," he told her.

(8) Kitty had repeated this without attaching any significance to the words. But her mother saw them in a different light. She knew that the old lady was expected from day to day, that she would be pleased at her son's choice, and she felt it strange that he should not make his offer through fear of vexing his mother. However, she was so anxious for the marriage itself, and still more for relief from her fears, that she believed it was so. Bitter as it was for the princess to see the unhappiness of her eldest daughter, Dolly, on the point of leaving her husband, her anxiety over the decision of her youngest daughter's fate engrossed all her feelings. Today, with Levin's reappearance, a fresh source of anxiety arose. She was afraid that her daughter, who had at one time, as she fancied, a feeling for Levin, might, from extreme sense of honor, refuse Vronsky, and that Levin's arrival might generally complicate and delay the affair so near being concluded.

(9) "Why, has he been here long?" the princess asked about Levin, as they returned home.

(10) "He came today, mamma."

(11) "There's one thing I want to say..." began the princess, and from her serious and alert face, Kitty guessed what it would be.

(12) "Mamma," she said, flushing hotly and turning quickly to her, "please, please don't say anything about that. I know, I know all about it."

(13) She wished for what her mother wished for, but the motives of her mother's wishes wounded her.

(14) "I only want to say that to raise hopes..."

(15) "Mamma, darling, for goodness' sake, don't talk about it. It's so horrible to talk about it."

(16) "I won't," said her mother, seeing the tears in her daughter's eyes; "but one thing, my love; you promised me you would have no secrets from me. You won't?"

(17) "Never, mamma, none," answered Kitty, flushing a little, and looking her mother straight in the face, "but there's no use in my telling you anything, and I...I...if I wanted to, I don't know what to say or how...I don't know..."

(18) "No, she could not tell an untruth with those eyes," thought the mother, smiling at her agitation and happiness. The princess smiled that what was taking place just now in her soul seemed to the poor child so immense and so important.

16. What is one difference between Levin and Count Vronsky?

a. Levin is shy and Count Vronsky has uncompromising opinions.
b. Levin is focused on life in the countryside while Count Vronsky has an aristocratic background.
c. Levin has uncompromising opinions while Count Vronsky is absorbed by cattle and peasants.
d. Levin is wealthy while Count Vronsky comes from an aristocratic family.

17. Read the following dictionary entry.

Fancy v. 1. To be interested in 2. To imagine something 3. To believe something that may or may not be true 4. To interpret something

Which definition best matches the way the word "fancied" is used in paragraph 8?

a. Definition 1
b. Definition 2
c. Definition 3
d. Definition 4

18. This story is set in Russia. Why is the location important to the story?

a. Princess Kitty is only interested in marrying a Russian
b. Princess Kitty will be matched according to the Russian style of using a matchmaker
c. The characters are, in part, shaped by their national heritage
d. Princess Kitty ultimately rebels against Russian society by choosing a husband using the English method

19. What is the likely importance of Vronsky's mother's arrival?

a. Vronsky is going to introduce his mother to Princess Kitty.
b. Vronsky is going to take his mother to a Moscow ball.
c. Vronsky is going to ask his mother if he should marry Kitty.
d. Vronsky is going to show his mother around Moscow.

20. In paragraph 6, the word "punctilious" most likely means:

a. careful
b. punctual
c. on time
d. jealous

21. Which sentence or phrase best demonstrates that customs in Moscow have changed?

a. The panics that had been lived through, the thoughts that had been brooded over, the money that had been wasted, and the disputes with her husband over marrying the two elder girls, Darya and Natalia!
b. She saw that girls of Kitty's age formed some sort of clubs, went to some sort of lectures, mixed freely in men's society
c. The French fashion—of the parents arranging their children's future—was not accepted
d. And so the princess was more uneasy over Kitty than she had been over her elder sisters.

22. Which sentence or phrase best illustrates why Kitty's mother thought Count Vronsky would be a good husband for Kitty?

a. When Vronsky appeared on the scene, she was still more delighted, confirmed in her opinion that Kitty was to make not simply a good, but a brilliant match.
b. She disliked in Levin his strange and uncompromising opinions and his shyness in society
c. Vronsky satisfied all the mother's desires.
d. Very wealthy, clever, or aristocratic family, on the highroad to a brilliant career in the army and at court, and a fascinating man.

23. What does the dialogue between Kitty and her mother in paragraphs 9-17 show?

a. The mother disapproves of Kitty's feelings for Levin
b. Kitty is in love with Vronsky
c. Kitty is in love with Levin
d. Kitty feels conflicted about Levin and Vronsky

This question has two parts. Answer Part A, then answer Part B.

24. Part A: In paragraph 6, Kitty's mother is concerned that Kitty might marry someone who is *unfit to be her husband*. What characteristic is Kitty's mother mostly like to think makes a suitor unfit?

a. Shyness
b. A member of the aristocracy
c. Cleverness
d. Obedient

Part B: In what paragraph does Kitty's mother state this concern?

a. Paragraph 2
b. Paragraph 3
c. Paragraph 5
d. Paragraph 6

25. The author uses paragraph 1 to:

a. introduce Princess Kitty's mother
b. introduce the central conflict of the passage
c. describe the Moscow balls
d. describe Levin and Count Vronsky

Questions 26 – 34 pertain to the following passages:

Great Britain and Her Queen

By Anne E. Keeling

Chapter I

The Girl-Queen and Her Kingdom

(1) Rather more than one mortal lifetime, as we average life in these later days, has elapsed since that June morning of 1837, when Victoria of England, then a fair young princess of eighteen, was roused from her tranquil sleep in the old palace at Kensington, and bidden to rise and meet the Primate, and his dignified associates the Lord Chamberlain and the royal physician, who "were come on business of state to the Queen"—words of startling import, for they meant that, while the royal maiden lay sleeping, the aged King, whose heiress she was, had passed into the deeper sleep of death. It is already an often-told story how promptly, on receiving that summons, the young Queen rose and came to meet her first homagers, standing before them in hastily assumed wrappings, her hair hanging loosely, her feet in slippers, but in all her hearing such royally firm composure as deeply impressed those heralds of her greatness, who noticed at the same moment that her eyes were full of tears. This little scene is not only charming and touching, it is very significant, suggesting a combination of such qualities as are not always found united: sovereign good sense and readiness, blending with quick, artless feeling that sought no disguise—such feeling as again betrayed itself when on her ensuing proclamation the new Sovereign had to meet her people face to face, and stood before them at her palace window, composed but sad, the tears running unchecked down her fair pale face.

(2) That rare spectacle of simple human emotion, at a time when a selfish or thoughtless spirit would have leaped in exultation, touched the heart of England deeply, and was rightly held of happy omen. The nation's feeling is aptly expressed in the glowing verse of Mrs. Browning, praying Heaven's blessing on the "weeping Queen," and prophesying for her the love, happiness, and honour which have been hers in no stinted measure. "Thou shalt be well beloved," said the poetess; there are very few sovereigns of whom it could be so truly said that they *have* been well beloved, for not many have so well deserved it. The faith of the singer has been amply justified, as time has made manifest the rarer qualities joyfully divined in those early days in the royal child, the single darling hope of the nation.

(3) Once before in the recent annals of our land had expectations and desires equally ardent centred themselves on one young head. Much of the loyal devotion which had been alienated from the immediate family of George III had transferred itself to his grandchild, the Princess Charlotte, sole offspring of the unhappy marriage between George, Prince of Wales, and Caroline of Brunswick. The people had watched with vivid interest the young romance of Princess Charlotte's happy marriage, and had bitterly lamented her too early death—an event which had overshadowed all English hearts with forebodings of disaster. Since that dark day a little of the old attachment of England to its sovereigns had revived for the frank-mannered sailor and "patriot king," William IV; but the hopes crushed by the death of the much-regretted Charlotte had renewed themselves with even better warrant for Victoria. She was the child of no ill-omened, miserable marriage, but of a fitting union; her parents had been sundered only by death, not by wretched domestic dissensions. People heard that the mortal malady which deprived her of a father had been brought about by the Duke of Kent's simple delight in his baby princess, which kept him playing with the child when he should have been changing his wet outdoor garb; and they found something touching and tender in the tragic little circumstance. And everything that could be noticed of the manner in which the bereaved duchess was training up her precious charge spoke well for the mother's wisdom and affection, and for the future of the daughter.

(4) It was indeed a happy day for England when Edward, Duke of Kent, the fourth son of George III, was wedded to Victoria of Saxe-Coburg, the widowed Princess of Leiningen—happy, not only because of the admirable skill with which that lady conducted her illustrious child's education, and because of the pure, upright principles, the frank, noble character, which she transmitted to that child, but because the family connection established through that marriage was to be yet further serviceable to the interests of our realm. Prince Albert of Saxe-Coburg was second son of the Duchess of Kent's eldest brother, and thus first cousin of the Princess Victoria—"the Mayflower," as, in fond allusion to the month of her birth, her mother's kinsfolk loved to call her: and it has been made plain that dreams of a possible union between the two young cousins, very nearly of an age, were early cherished by the elders who loved and admired both.

(5) The Princess's life, however, was sedulously guarded from all disturbing influences. She grew up in healthy simplicity and seclusion; she was not apprised of her nearness to the throne till she was twelve years old; she had been little at Court, little in sight, but had been made familiar with her own land and its history, having received the higher education so essential to her great position; while simple truth and rigid honesty were the very atmosphere of her existence. From such a training much might be hoped; but even those who knew most and hoped most were not quite prepared for the strong individual character and power of self-determination that revealed themselves in the girlish being so suddenly transferred "from the nursery to the throne." It was quickly noticed that the part of Queen and mistress seemed native to her, and that she filled it with not more grace than propriety. "She always strikes me as possessed of singular penetration, firmness, and independence," wrote Dr. Norman Macleod in 1860; acute observers in 1837 took note of the same traits, rarer far in youth than in full maturity, and closely connected with the "reasoning, searching" quality of her mind, "anxious to get at the root and reality of things, and abhorring all shams, whether in word or deed."

(6) It was well for England that its young Sovereign could exemplify virile strength as well as womanly sweetness; for it was indeed a cloudy and dark day when she was called to her post of lonely grandeur and hard responsibility; and to fill that post rightly would have overtasked and overwhelmed a feebler nature. It is true that the peace of Europe, won at Waterloo, was still unbroken. But already, within our borders and without them, there were the signs of coming storm. The condition of Ireland was chronically bad; the condition of England was full of danger; on the Continent a new period of earth-shaking revolution announced itself not doubtfully.

(7) It would be hardly possible to exaggerate the wretched state of the sister isle, where fires of recent hate were still smouldering, and where the poor inhabitants, guilty and guiltless, were daily living on the verge of famine, over which they were soon to be driven. Their ill condition much aggravated by the intemperate habits to which despairing men so easily fall a prey. The expenditure of Ireland on proof spirits alone had in the year 1829 attained the sum of £6,000,000.

(8) In England many agricultural labourers were earning starvation wages, were living on bad and scanty food, and were housed so wretchedly that they might envy the hounds their dry and clean kennels. A dark symptom of their hungry discontent had shown itself in the strange crime of rick-burning, which went on under cloud of night season after season, despite the utmost precautions which the luckless farmers could adopt. The perpetrators were not dimly guessed to be half-famished creatures, taking a mad revenge for their wretchedness by destroying the tantalising stores of grain, too costly for their consumption; the price of wheat in the early years of Her Majesty's reign and for some time previously being very high, and reaching at one moment (1847) the extraordinary figure of a hundred and two shillings per quarter.

(9) There was threatening distress, too, in some parts of the manufacturing districts; in others a tolerably high level of wages indicated prosperity. But even in the more favoured districts there was needless suffering. The hours of work, unrestricted by law, were cruelly long; nor did there exist any restriction as to the employment of operatives of very tender years. "The cry of the children" was rising up to heaven, not from the factory only, but from the underground darkness of the mine, where a system of pitiless infant slavery prevailed, side by side with the employment of women as beasts of burden, "in an atmosphere of filth and profligacy." The condition of too many toilers was rendered more hopeless by the thriftless follies born of ignorance. The educational provision made by the piety of former ages was no longer adequate to the needs of the ever-growing nation; and all the voluntary efforts made by clergy and laity, by Churchmen and Dissenters, did not fill up the deficiency—a fact which had only just begun to meet with State recognition. It was in 1834 that Government first obtained from Parliament the grant of a small sum in aid of education. Under a defective system of poor-relief, recently reformed, an immense mass of idle pauperism had come into being; it still remained to be seen if a new Poor Law could do away with the mischief created by the old one.

(10) Looking at the earliest years of Her Majesty's rule, the first impulse is to exclaim:

(11) "And all this trouble did not pass, but grew."

26. Which of these is NOT one of the immediate problems that faced the nation at the time that Victoria was crowned?

a. Europe was not at war.
b. The people in Ireland were suffering.
c. Agricultural laborers were not earning enough money.
d. There wasn't enough money for education.

27. What is paragraph 3 mainly about?

a. Victoria's childhood
b. The royal family
c. Victoria's cousin
d. Victoria's father, the Duke of Kent

28. In paragraph 2, the author uses a quote from Mrs. Browning to show which of the following?

a. Queen Victoria was not beloved
b. Queen Victoria had a lot of happiness in her life
c. Mrs. Browning accurately predicted the people's opinion about Queen Victoria
d. Queen Victoria had a selfish and thoughtless spirit

This question has two parts. Answer Part A, then answer Part B.

29. Part A: The primary purpose of paragraphs 7-9 is to:

a. illustrate Queen Victoria's first acts as queen
b. show the poor conditions for workers in manufacturing districts
c. show the problems faced by the people of Ireland
d. describe the challenges faced by Victoria when she became queen

Part B: Give a sentence from the passage that supports your answer in Part A.

____

____

____

30. According to the author, what was one specific problem that resulted from the government's efforts to aid the poor?

a. Poverty increased
b. There wasn't enough money for education
c. The trouble grew
d. The system was reformed

31. What is one reason why Victoria's childhood was relatively simple?

a. She spent much of her childhood with her cousin
b. She didn't know she had a possibility of being queen until she was twelve
c. She was very independent
d. She received a lot of education

32. Despite the despair expressed in paragraph 11, the reader can infer which of the below?

a. Queen Victoria was not able to solve any of the problems facing the nation
b. Queen Victoria was successful in solving many of the problems facing the nation
c. The people disliked Queen Victoria's rule
d. The troubles overwhelmed Queen Victoria

33. Why is it significant that observers in 1837 noticed the same character traits in Queen Victoria as Dr. Macleod noticed in 1860?

a. Victoria had positive traits throughout her reign.
b. The traits caused problems throughout Queen Victoria's reign.
c. The traits consistently increased the anxiety of Queen Victoria's subjects.
d. The observations show that Queen Victoria's subjects were consistently displeased with her.

34. Which of these best shows Victoria's feelings on the day she was crowned queen?

a. The young Queen rose and came to meet her first homagers, standing before them in hastily assumed wrappings, her hair hanging loosely, her feet in slippers
b. Suggesting a combination of such qualities as are not always found united
c. Sovereign good sense and readiness
d. Composed but sad, the tears running unchecked down her fair pale face

Questions 35 – 37 pertain to both Anna Karenina and Great Britain and her Queen:

35. What do Princess Kitty and Queen Victoria have in common?

a. They both have close relationships with their mothers.
b. They both struggle to rule a nation.
c. They are expected to follow society's rules for behavior.
d. They live in an environment with rigid and high expectations.

36. What is one difference between Queen Victoria and Princess Kitty, as they are described in the passages?

a. Princess Kitty is concerned with her own future while Queen Victoria is concerned with her nation's future.
b. Princess Kitty is concerned about the changing traditions in Russia while Queen Victoria is not seeking to change things in Great Britain.
c. Princess Kitty lives in Russia, which does not have major problems, while Queen Victoria's nation, England, faces many challenges.
d. Princess Kitty is concerned about Russian society while Queen Victoria is concerned about preparing herself to be queen.

37. Both selections end on a note of:

a. optimism
b. uncertainty
c. hope
d. despair

Use the following visual representation to answer questions 38 -40:

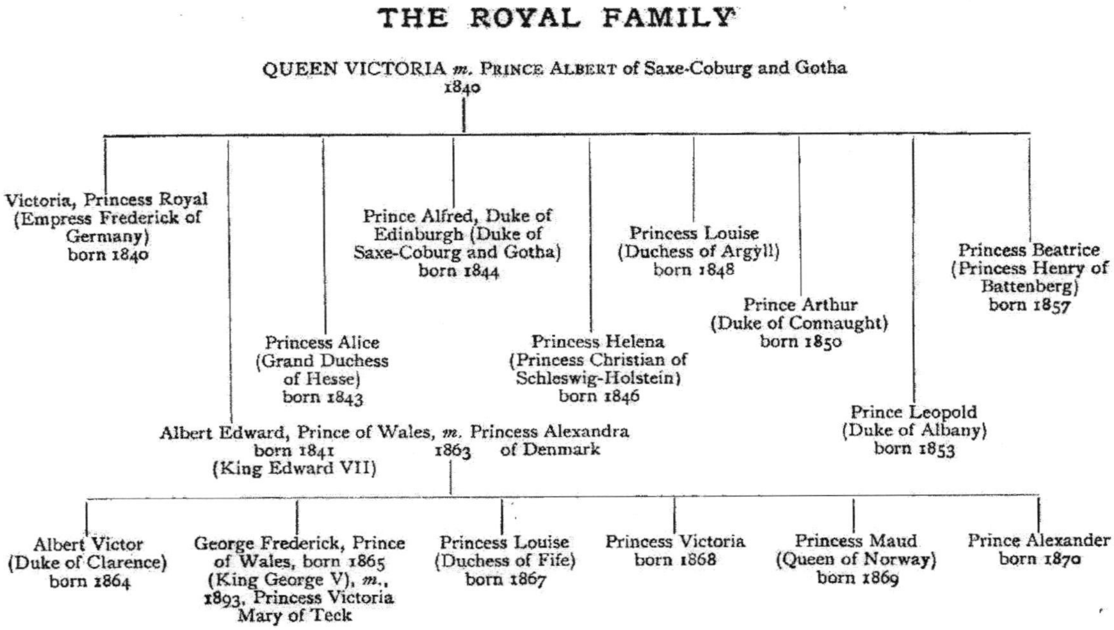

38. What title is most likely used for Great Britain's future king or queen?

a. Duke of Albany
b. Princess Henry of Battenberg
c. Queen of Norway
d. Prince of Wales

39. What is the most likely reason why the diagram only shows the children of Albert Edward and Alexandra?

a. Queen Victoria and Prince Albert didn't consider the other children to be important.
b. The author only wanted to show the succession to the British throne.
c. The author wanted to show when Queen Victoria's namesake, Princess Victoria, was born.
d. The author didn't have room for other children.

40. In what way is the family tree organized?

a. The oldest generation at the bottom, and the youngest generation at the top.
b. The youngest children on right and the oldest children on the left.
c. The youngest children on the left and the oldest children on the right.
d. The grandparents (Queen Victoria and Prince Albert) are on the top, followed by their children, grandchildren, and great-grandchildren on the bottom layers.

Short-Answer Question

How do Kitty's feelings about Levin concern her mother? Explain your answer and support it with evidence from the selection?

Answers and Explanations

1. A: Emma's life had been marked by the comfort of consistency, a close relationship with Miss Taylor, and the knowledge she tended to get her own way. Miss Taylor's marriage upsets that comfort and consistency because a major aspect of Emma's life will change. Emma is afraid her intellect will be stifled without Miss Taylor, so she does not approach the change as an opportunity for possible intellectual growth.

2. Part A: D: The author uses words such as comfortable and happy to describe Emma's first twenty-one years. During this time, little vexed her. Based on this context, you can conclude that *vex* has the opposite meaning of words such as comfortable and happy. The answer choice most different from these positive words is displease.

Part B: A: In the excerpt it says "distress or vex" which tells you that the meaning of "vex" is similar to the meaning of distress.

3. C: The author states that Emma possesses the "power of having rather too much her own way," and instead of feeling happy for her recently married friend, she feels sorry for herself. These descriptions characterize Emma as selfish. Emma may consider herself unfortunate following Miss Taylor's marriage, but a lifetime of privilege and having her own way hardly makes her an unfortunate character. While Emma may indeed prove to be devious, this excerpt offers no evidence of deviousness. Although Emma seems to value intellectual interaction, nothing in the excerpt implies that she is particularly studious.

4. B: A product of upper-class privilege, Emma has grown accustomed always to getting her way When Miss Taylor's marriage disrupts this aspect of her life, Emma cannot deal with the situation in a mature fashion and instead sinks into self-pity and sorrow. Although Emma cannot enjoy Miss Taylor's happiness upon her wedding because Emma is so wrapped up in her own feelings, this does not mean she feels neither kindness nor love for her friend.

5. B: The color black is often used figuratively to suggest badness. Emma is sad about Miss Taylor's wedding, and enduring the event has become nothing more than "black work" to her. Perhaps she pretends she is happy about the wedding, but no evidence in this excerpt suggests this conclusion. In addition, no evidence in the excerpt suggests that Emma organized the wedding. The author does not use "black" as a literal color in this excerpt, and no evidence in the excerpt suggests the wedding party wears black clothing.

6. D: By beginning his argument with an immediate criticism of the existing federal government, he immediately portrays it as a system in need of improvement. By presenting the government's inefficacy in no uncertain terms, Hamilton assumes the reader will take his claim at face value and be convinced of his subsequent argument for improvements. Hamilton only criticizes the federal government explicitly; he does not criticize the Constitution.

7. A: By addressing the reader directly and uniting himself with the reader by using words such as "we," Hamilton is establishing a sense of agreement between himself and the reader. By doing so he wants the reader to believe he and the reader share the same desires for and concerns about America. The first-person point of view does not necessarily establish a friendly or informal tone.

8. C: Alexander Hamilton describes his opponents as loud and bitter in this sentence. Such words suggest a lack of rationality, self-control, and kindness. This word usage almost represents an attempt to portray his political opponents as less than human Hamilton is seeking to strengthen his argument by suggesting those oppose his argument are angry and irrational.

9. B: In paragraph 3, Alexander Hamilton attacks politicians who fear any change resulting from the Constitution that might diminish their power. Although this attack may be central to his argument, Hamilton does not want to leave the reader with the bitter feeling that Hamilton's sole reason for writing is to attack his opponents. Ironically, he then continues his attacks for the remainder of the excerpt.

10. A: According to the writer, a tyrant would start by pretending to be submissive to the will of the people (that is, paying court to the people) to gain popularity, then abuse his or her newfound power. Based on this context, you can conclude that "obsequious" and "submissive" share the same meaning.

11. B: In the opening paragraph of his second inaugural address, Lincoln discusses his first address, describing how the first actions in the coming Civil War were just beginning to take place. The country had suffered much since then as the war got underway and continued throughout his first term as president. This change in the nation inspired the plea for an end to the hostilities that dominates his second inaugural address.

12. C: Lincoln believed that the South was wrong for making war by trying to secede from the Union, and the North was right for trying to maintain the Union by refusing to accept the hostile action. This quote shows he believed the actions of the North were more justifiable than those of the South.

13. A: Lincoln states that "if God wills that it [the war] continue ... until every drop of blood drawn with the lash shall be paid by another drawn with the sword, as was said three thousand years ago, so still it must be said 'the judgments of the Lord are true and righteous altogether.'" This statement indicates Lincoln's belief that the war was a product of God's will.

14. D: Lincoln delivered his Second Inaugural Address after a time of great hardship for the United States: the Civil War. His plea for the country's resolution of its severe problems must have been an emotional experience for the president, and his voice must have conveyed this emotionality as he read the speech. As a result, reading the document online could not have quite the same emotional impact as hearing it in person.

15. C: Lincoln's final paragraph issues a plea for "malice toward none, with charity for all." This statement represents an attempt to heal the pain that existed between the North and South during the Civil War. Lincoln wants the United States to reunite and move on from the war as a solid, individual, caring nation.

16. B: because the passage says in paragraph 3 that Levin is absorbed in cattle and peasants, which can be found in the countryside. Paragraph 4 states that Vronsky comes from an aristocratic background, or family. While it's true that Levin is shy, choice A is incorrect because Levin is the character who has uncompromising opinions, not Vronsky. Choice C is incorrect because it is Levin who is absorbed by cattle and peasants, not Vronsky. Choice D is incorrect because paragraph 4 states that Vronsky is wealthy, not Levin.

17. C: because the context of the sentence shows that Kitty's mother believed, or fancied, that Kitty had feelings for Levin. While it might also be true that Kitty fancies (or is interested in Levin), choice A is incorrect because the structure of the sentence shows that *fancied* is used to show the mother's opinion. Choice C is incorrect because Kitty's mother is not imagining Kitty's feelings; based on Kitty's behavior earlier, she believes that Kitty was in love with Levin. Choice D is incorrect because Kitty's mother is not interpreting current events; instead, she fancies that Kitty had feelings for Levin based on her observations of Kitty's past behavior.

18. C: is the correct answer because Kitty's mother is torn by the changes that are reshaping her society. The reader can best understand the impact of these changes by understanding original Russian society, which is partly explained in paragraphs 1 and 6. Choice A is incorrect because the passage does not present evidence that Kitty is only interested in marrying a Russian; while this may be true, the passage does not indicate Kitty's feelings. Choice B is incorrect because paragraph 6 states that the Russian style of matchmaking was unseemly and no longer used. Choice D is incorrect because the reader does not yet know whom Kitty will marry or whether Kitty will use the English method by choosing her husband herself.

19. C: that Vronsky is going to ask his mother if he should marry Kitty. Paragraph 7 says that Vronsky never makes important decisions without consulting his mother, and her visit will be an opportunity for him to ask her important questions. Choice A is incorrect because the passage doesn't indicate that Kitty might meet Vronsky's mother. Choice B is incorrect because Vronsky attends balls to dance with Kitty, not his mother. While Vronsky might show his mother around Moscow, choice D is incorrect because the passage does not imply that this will happen.

20. A: because the rest of the sentence explains that Kitty's father is punctilious about his daughters' honor and reputation, which means that he's careful to guard them. Choice B is incorrect because *punctual* means to be on time, and the passage doesn't show Kitty's father attempting to arrive anywhere promptly. Choice C is incorrect because it has the same meaning as punctual. Choice D is incorrect because *jealous* is used in the following sentence and is used to show that he guards his daughters carefully.

21. B: because it gives specific details about new behaviors, such as forming clubs and going to lectures. Choice A is incorrect because it focuses on the stress Kitty's mother felt as Kitty's older daughters got married. Choice C is incorrect because it shows that the French fashion was not accepted; this means that Russian society has not changed to embrace the French fashion. Choice D is incorrect because it shows Kitty's mother is increasingly uneasy but does not show why.

22. D: because this answer shows the specific attributes that Kitty's mother likes about Vronsky, such as wealth and cleverness. Choice A is incorrect because it only states that Kitty's mother likes Vronsky; however, this choice does not explain why. Choice B is incorrect because it shows that Kitty's mother dislikes Levin without explaining why she likes Vronsky. Choice C is incorrect because it simply states that Kitty's mother likes Vronsky.

23. D: is the correct answer because Kitty shows her inner conflict without even mentioning Levin or Vronsky's names. However, Kitty clearly shows her distress, such as when she cries in paragraph 16 and says, "It's so horrible," in paragraph 15. Choice A is incorrect because the mother doesn't express her opinion during the dialogue; instead, she's simply trying to understand how Kitty's feeling. Choices B and C are incorrect because Kitty doesn't express her feelings for either Levin or Vronsky; at this point in the story, she is very conflicted.

24. Part A: because paragraph 3 says that Kitty's mother dislikes Levin's shyness. Choices B and C are incorrect because these are the characteristics mentioned in paragraph 4 as positive traits that Vronsky has. Even though Vronsky, the mother's favorite, is very obedient to his mother, Kitty's mother does say that this trait makes him unsuitable for Kitty. She is a little uneasy about this trait, but does not rule Vronsky out as an acceptable husband. Therefore, choice D is incorrect.

Part B: B: In paragraph 3, Kitty's mother says that she dislikes Levin's shyness.

25. B: because the paragraph shows that the central conflict is Kitty's feelings about Levin and Vronsky. Choice A is incorrect because Kitty's mother does not appear prominently in paragraph 1.

Choice C is incorrect because the paragraph only mentions the balls but does not give any details. Choice D is incorrect because the reader only learns details about Levin and Vronsky in the following paragraphs, not in paragraph 1.

26. A: because paragraph 6 explains that the peace that came upon Europe after the battle of Waterloo was still unbroken; the continent was not at war. Choices B, C, and D are incorrect because paragraphs 7-9 explain that these choices were problems. Paragraph 7 talks about the problems in Ireland, paragraph 8 talks about the low, or starvation, wages earned by many agricultural workers, and paragraph 9 mentions the problems with the education system.

27. B: because the paragraph talks primarily about the royal family, including George III and Princess Charlotte. This paragraph serves to partially explain how Victoria came to be queen. Choice A is incorrect because the paragraph gives few details about Victoria's childhood. Instead, it talks about her father and other royals. Choice C is incorrect because paragraph 4, not paragraph 3, talks about Albert, Victoria's cousin. Choice D is incorrect because only a portion of the paragraph discusses the Duke of Kent. The paragraph is mainly about the royal family as a whole.

28. C: is the correct answer because the paragraph shows that Mrs. Browning predicted that the people would love Victoria and that the people did, ultimately, love her (the paragraph says "there are very few sovereigns of whom it could be so truly said that they *have* been well beloved"). Choice A is incorrect because it is the opposite of how the people felt about her. Choice B is incorrect because the quote does not mention any poets other than Mrs. Browning. Choice D is incorrect because the passage does not state that Queen Victoria had those characteristics.

29. Part A: D: is the correct answer because the paragraphs give many details about the troubles that faced the nation when Victoria became queen. Choice A is incorrect because they don't describe what Queen Victoria did to address these problems. Choices B and C are incorrect because the paragraphs discuss many problems, not just those specific problems.

Part B: Any sentence that showed some of the troubles that the nation was facing when Queen Victoria took over would be correct. Example sentence: In England many agricultural labourers were earning starvation wages, were living on bad and scanty food, and were housed so wretchedly that they might envy the hounds their dry and clean kennels.

30. A: because paragraph 9 states that the system of poor-relief was defective, leading to an immense amount of poverty. Choice B is incorrect because the lack of funding for education is presented as a separate problem from the efforts to aid the poor. Choice C is incorrect because it is not specific and could apply to many of the problems described in paragraphs 7-9. Choice D is incorrect because the government had already reformed the poor-relief system in a failed attempt to solve the problems, and we have not yet seen whether new reforms are coming.

31. B: because paragraph 5 says that Victoria did not know how close she was to the throne until she was twelve years old. This supports the author's point earlier in the sentence that her childhood was simple. Choice A is incorrect because the passage never says she spent time with her cousin; instead, paragraph 4 simply describes Prince Albert's lineage. Choice C is incorrect because the author does not indicate that Victoria's independence is related to her simplicity. Choice D is incorrect because the passage does not imply that the education caused her childhood to be simple. Instead, the education prepared her for the throne.

32. B: because the reader knows from paragraph 2 that Queen Victoria was beloved. The reader can infer that she would not have been beloved if she had been unable to improve life for her subjects. Choice A is incorrect due to the reader's assumption from paragraph 2 that Victoria solved some of the problems was therefore well-loved by the people. Choice C is incorrect because the reader can infer that Victoria faced many challenges, but the reader already knows that people liked her rule. Choice D is incorrect because the high-regard with which the people gave Queen Victoria shows that the troubles likely didn't overwhelm her.

33. A: because the traits described by Dr. Macleod are positive traits that contributed to the queen's strengths. Since they were observed both in 1837 and 1860, the reader can infer that the queen had these traits throughout her reign. Choice B is incorrect because the traits described are positive; the passage does not indicate that they caused problems. Choice C is incorrect because Dr. Macleod and the other observers seem to admire these traits, which means they did not cause anxiety. Choice D is incorrect because the traits are positive traits, which means that Queen Victoria's subjects were unlikely to be displeased.

34. D: because the word *composed* shows Victoria's inner strength and calm while her tears show her sadness. Choice A is incorrect because it describes her appearance rather than her inner state. Choice B is incorrect because it discusses her qualities without mentioning specific qualities that might show Victoria's feelings. Choice C is incorrect because it describes Victoria's specific qualities or personality traits but not her emotions on the day she was crowned.

35. D: because both Kitty and Victoria are in an environment with high, although different, expectations. Kitty is expected to make a good match, and the passage implies that this is highly important. Victoria is expected to fix the problems in England. Choice A is incorrect because the reader only learns about Kitty's relationship with her mother. No information is given about Victoria's mother. Choice B is incorrect because only Victoria has to rule. Kitty is a princess, but the passage does not indicate that she is in power. Choice C is incorrect because no information is given in *Great Britain and her Queen* about the behavioral rules that Victoria should have followed. The passage focuses more on her traits and the challenges she will face as queen.

36. A: is the correct answer because *Anna Karenina* is about Kitty's personal life while *Great Britain and her Queen* is about Queen Victoria's struggle to rule a nation. Choice B is incorrect because Kitty is not concerned about changing traditions in Russia; her mother is the one who is concerned. Furthermore, Queen Victoria must change things in Great Britain; the passage outlines several problems that must be solved. Choice C is incorrect because *Anna Karenina* does not indicate whether or not Russia has major problems; therefore, the reader does not have enough information to determine if this is true. Choice D is incorrect because Kitty's mother, not Kitty, is concerned about Russian society. Furthermore, the reader doesn't see Victoria's concern; the reader only sees the author's concern.

37. B: because both passages end by alluding to an uncertain future. At the end of *Anna Karenina,* neither Kitty nor her mother knows whom Kitty is going to marry. *Great Britain and her Queen* ends with an uncertain sense of how the new queen is going to tackle the many problems that face the nation. Choice A is incorrect because the reader does not see an optimistic future in either passage. For example, *Great Britain and her Queen* ends after describing all of Britain's problems. Choice C is incorrect for the same reasons; the passages end with uncertainty for the future rather than hope. While *Great Britain and her Queen* also ends with some despair, choice D is incorrect because there is no sense of despair in *Anna Karenina.* Kitty is upset because she's not sure what to do, not because she is despairing.

38. D: because two people labeled as Prince of Wales on the family tree are also marked as king. Albert Edward was King Edward VII, and George Frederick was King George V. Choices A and B are incorrect because Princess Beatrice and Prince Leopold only have one title listed, and it's not king or queen. Choice C is incorrect because Princess Maud was the queen of Norway, not Great Britain.

39. B: is the correct answer because the family tree shows the children of Queen Victoria and then the children of King Edward VII. Since no other children are shown, the reader can infer that the author only wanted to show the children of the queen or king. Choice A is incorrect because the reader does not have any information about how Queen Victoria and Prince Albert felt about their children. However, the reader does have information about the line of succession. Choice C is incorrect because if the author only wanted to show Princess Victoria, he could have left out Queen Victoria's other children and grand-children. Choice D is incorrect because the author could have found a way to organize the diagram to make room for other children (for example, the author organized the placement of Queen Victoria's children in order to make room for all of them). It is more likely that the author was most interested in showing the line of succession.

40. B: is the correct answer because the birthdates show that the youngest children are on the right and their older siblings are on the left side of the family tree. Choice A is incorrect because Queen Victoria and Prince Albert are the oldest generation, and they are at the top of the family tree. Choice C is incorrect because the youngest children are on the right, not the left (the reader can see this by looking at the birthdates). Choice D is partially correct because Queen Victoria and Prince Albert are at the top of the family tree, but the family tree does not show great-grandchildren. Although it looks like there are more than three layers, the middle layers all show Queen Victoria and Prince Albert's children.

Sample Short Answer Response

> Kitty's mother is concerned about Kitty's feelings for Levin throughout the passage. Paragraph 2 shows that Kitty's mother, who is called "the princess", is not happy that Kitty is dating Levin. She doesn't state this unhappiness directly; instead, she beats around the bush and "maintained that Kitty was too young, that Levin had done nothing to prove that he had serious intentions..." Kitty's mother is looking for every possible reason to believe that Kitty does not love Levin. After Levin leaves Moscow, Kitty's mother is relieved that he is out of Kitty's life. She's happy that Kitty is now interested in Vronsky. For example, paragraph 4 says, "Vronsky satisfied all the mother's desires." Kitty's mother thinks that Kitty will just marry Vronsky, but once Levin returns in paragraph 8, she is very anxious again. This time, she's worried that Kitty will insist on marrying Levin out of a sense of honor, because she loved him first, rather than because she continues to love him. Kitty's mother ends the passage by continuing to hope that Kitty will choose Vronsky.

Practice Test #2

Practice Questions

Questions 1-5 pertain to the following excerpt.

Excerpt from Wuthering Heights

By Emily Brontë

Chapter 1

(1) 1801.—I have just returned from a visit to my landlord—the solitary neighbour that I shall be troubled with. This is certainly a beautiful country! In all England, I do not believe that I could have fixed on a situation so completely removed from the stir of society. A perfect misanthropist's heaven: and Mr. Heathcliff and I are such a suitable pair to divide the desolation between us. A capital fellow! He little imagined how my heart warmed towards him when I beheld his black eyes withdraw so suspiciously under their brows, as I rode up, and when his fingers sheltered themselves, with a jealous resolution, still further in his waistcoat, as I announced my name.

(2) "Mr. Heathcliff?" I said. A nod was the answer.

(3) "Mr. Lockwood, your new tenant, sir. I do myself the honour of calling as soon as possible after my arrival, to express the hope that I have not inconvenienced you by my perseverance in soliciting the occupation of Thrushcross Grange: I heard yesterday you had had some thoughts—"

(4) "Thrushcross Grange is my own, sir," he interrupted, wincing. "I should not allow any one to inconvenience me, if I could hinder it—walk in!"

(5) The "walk in" was uttered with closed teeth, and expressed the sentiment, "Go to the Deuce:" even the gate over which he leant manifested no sympathizing movement to the words; and I think that circumstance determined me to accept the invitation: I felt interested in a man who seemed more exaggeratedly reserved than myself.

(6) When he saw my horse's breast fairly pushing the barrier, he did put out his hand to unchain it, and then sullenly preceded me up the causeway, calling, as we entered the court—"Joseph, take Mr. Lockwood's horse; and bring up some wine."

(7) "Here we have the whole establishment of domestics, I suppose," was the reflection suggested by this compound order. "No wonder the grass grows up between the flags, and cattle are the only hedge-cutters."

(8) Joseph was an elderly, nay, an old man: very old, perhaps, though hale and sinewy. "The Lord help us!" he soliloquized in an undertone of peevish displeasure, while relieving me of my horse: looking, meantime, in my face so sourly that I charitably conjectured he must have need of divine aid to digest his dinner, and his pious ejaculation had no reference to my unexpected advent.

(9) Wuthering Heights is the name of Mr. Heathcliff's dwelling. "Wuthering" being a significant provincial adjective, descriptive of the atmospheric tumult to which its station is exposed in stormy weather. Pure, bracing ventilation they must have up there at all times, indeed: one may guess the power of the north wind blowing over the edge, by the excessive slant of a few stunted firs at the end of the house; and by a range of gaunt thorns all stretching their limbs one way, as if craving alms of the sun. Happily, the architect had foresight to build it strong: the narrow windows are deeply set in the wall, and the corners defended with large jutting stones.

(10) Before passing the threshold, I paused to admire a quantity of grotesque carving lavished over the front, and especially about the principal door; above which, among a wilderness of crumbling griffins and shameless little boys, I detected the date "1500," and the name "Hareton Earnshaw.'" I would have made a few comments, and requested a short history of the place from the surly owner; but his attitude at the door appeared to demand my speedy entrance, or complete departure, and I had no desire to aggravate his impatience previous to inspecting the penetralium.

1. What is the author's purpose in describing Wuthering Heights in such detail?

a. to explain why Mr. Lockwood is so delighted by the house
b. to prove that Heathcliff is a misanthrope
c. to show how all houses looked in the 1500s
d. to establish a strange and foreboding tone

2. Which line from the excerpt helps establish a somewhat sarcastic tone?

a. ... Mr. Heathcliff and I are such a suitable pair to divide the desolation between us.
b. ... I charitably conjectured he must have need of divine aid to digest his dinner...
c. ... the narrow windows are deeply set in the wall, and the corners defended with large jutting stones.
d. ... his attitude at the door appeared to demand my speedy entrance...

3. As it is used in paragraph 9, what does the word "bracing" mean?

a. supporting
b. bracketing
c. staying.
d. invigorating

4. What does Heathcliff mean in paragraph 7 when he says, "cattle are the only hedge-cutters"?

a. Heathcliff is mad and believes his cattle are capable of gardening.
b. Heathcliff is irritated by how the cattle destroy the vegetation on his property.
c. The only way his property will be landscaped is if cattle decide to eat the hedges.
d. The hedges that grow on Heathcliff's property are particularly delicious to cattle.

5. Although now regarded as a classic, Wuthering Heights received some harsh reviews when published in 1847. Based on this excerpt, what might have been one of the most common criticisms?

a. The characters are not particularly likable.
b. Emily Bronte misuses language.
c. The plot is completely unoriginal.
d. Emily Bronte fails to describe the characters.

Questions 6-10 pertain to the following excerpt.

Excerpt from Act 1, Scene 1 of A Midsummer Night's Dream

By William Shakespeare

Enter EGEUS, HERMIA, LYSANDER, and DEMETRIUS

EGEUS: Happy be Theseus, our renowned duke!

THESEUS: Thanks, good Egeus: what's the news with thee?

EGEUS: Full of vexation come I, with complaint

Against my child, my daughter Hermia.

Stand forth, Demetrius. My noble lord,

This man hath my consent to marry her.

Stand forth, Lysander: and my gracious duke,

This man hath bewitch'd the bosom of my child;

Thou, thou, Lysander, thou hast given her rhymes,

And interchanged love-tokens with my child:

Thou hast by moonlight at her window sung,

With feigning voice verses of feigning love,

And stolen the impression of her fantasy

With bracelets of thy hair, rings, gawds, conceits,

Knacks, trifles, nosegays, sweetmeats, messengers

Of strong prevailment in unharden'd youth:

With cunning hast thou filch'd my daughter's heart,

Turn'd her obedience, which is due to me,

To stubborn harshness: and, my gracious duke,

Be it so she; will not here before your grace

Consent to marry with Demetrius,
I beg the ancient privilege of Athens,
As she is mine, I may dispose of her:
Which shall be either to this gentleman
Or to her death, according to our law
Immediately provided in that case.
THESEUS: What say you, Hermia? be advised fair maid:
To you your father should be as a god;
One that composed your beauties, yea, and one
To whom you are but as a form in wax
By him imprinted and within his power
To leave the figure or disfigure it.
Demetrius is a worthy gentleman.
HERMIA: So is Lysander.
THESEUS: In himself he is;
But in this kind, wanting your father's voice,
The other must be held the worthier.
HERMIA: I would my father look'd but with my eyes.
THESEUS: Rather your eyes must with his judgment look.
HERMIA: I do entreat your grace to pardon me.
I know not by what power I am made bold,
Nor how it may concern my modesty,
In such a presence here to plead my thoughts;
But I beseech your grace that I may know
The worst that may befall me in this case,
If I refuse to wed Demetrius.
THESEUS: Either to die the death or to abjure
For ever the society of men.

Therefore, fair Hermia, question your desires;

Know of your youth, examine well your blood,

Whether, if you yield not to your father's choice,

You can endure the livery of a nun,

For aye to be in shady cloister mew'd,

To live a barren sister all your life,

Chanting faint hymns to the cold fruitless moon.

Thrice-blessed they that master so their blood,

To undergo such maiden pilgrimage;

But earthlier happy is the rose distill'd,

Than that which withering on the virgin thorn

Grows, lives and dies in single blessedness.

HERMIA: So will I grow, so live, so die, my lord,

Ere I will my virgin patent up

Unto his lordship, whose unwished yoke

My soul consents not to give sovereignty.

THESEUS: Take time to pause; and, by the nest new moon--

The sealing-day betwixt my love and me,

For everlasting bond of fellowship--

Upon that day either prepare to die

For disobedience to your father's will,

Or else to wed Demetrius, as he would;

Or on Diana's altar to protest

For aye austerity and single life.

DEMETRIUS: Relent, sweet Hermia: and, Lysander, yield

Thy crazed title to my certain right.

LYSANDER: You have her father's love, Demetrius;

Let me have Hermia's: do you marry him.

EGEUS: Scornful Lysander! true, he hath my love,
And what is mine my love shall render him.
And she is mine, and all my right of her
I do estate unto Demetrius.
LYSANDER: I am, my lord, as well derived as he,
As well possess'd; my love is more than his;
My fortunes every way as fairly rank'd,
If not with vantage, as Demetrius';
And, which is more than all these boasts can be,
I am beloved of beauteous Hermia:
Why should not I then prosecute my right?
Demetrius, I'll avouch it to his head,
Made love to Nedar's daughter, Helena,
And won her soul; and she, sweet lady, dotes,
Devoutly dotes, dotes in idolatry,
Upon this spotted and inconstant man.
THESEUS: I must confess that I have heard so much,
And with Demetrius thought to have spoke thereof;
But, being over-full of self-affairs,
My mind did lose it. But, Demetrius, come;
And come, Egeus; you shall go with me,
I have some private schooling for you both.
For you, fair Hermia, look you arm yourself
To fit your fancies to your father's will;
Or else the law of Athens yields you up--
Which by no means we may extenuate--
To death, or to a vow of single life.
Come, my Hippolyta: what cheer, my love?

Demetrius and Egeus, go along:

I must employ you in some business

Against our nuptial and confer with you

Of something nearly that concerns yourselves.

EGEUS: With duty and desire we follow you.

Exeunt all but LYSANDER and HERMIA

6. At the end of this excerpt, everyone exits except for Lysander and Hermia. Why might the writer allow these two characters to remain in the scene together?

a. Lysander and Hermia decide to end their relationship during the excerpt and will say their final goodbyes when left alone together.
b. Lysander and Hermia are not included in Theseus's request that Demetrious, Egeus, and Hippolyta follow him elsewhere.
c. Lysander and Hermia are the two main characters of the play and therefore are expected to share a number of scenes together.
d. Lysander and Hermia are in love and will discuss how their relationship will proceed after the other characters leave.

7. Which of the following does Egeus NOT accuse Lysander of doing?

a. giving gifts to Hermia
b. singing to Hermia
c. writing poetry for Hermia
d. painting a portrait of Hermia

8. A Midsummer Night's Dream deals with the themes of true love and mismatched relationships. In what way are these themes paralleled in Lysander and Demetrius?

a. Both love women who do not love them.
b. Both love women they know are not right for them.
c. Both love women they are not supposed to marry.
d. Both love women who are unaware of the men who love them.

9. Which line from the excerpt proves Hermia's willingness to pursue her relationship with Lysander no matter the cost?

a. I beseech your grace that I may know / The worst that may befall me in this case, / If I refuse to wed Demetrius
b. I do entreat your grace to pardon me. / I know not by what power I am made bold, / Nor how it may concern my modesty
c. Know of your youth, examine well your blood, / Whether, if you yield not to your father's choice, / You can endure the livery of a nun
d. Unto his lordship, whose unwished yoke / My soul consents not to give sovereignty

10. Nathaniel Hawthorne's novel The Scarlett Letter deals with a romantic relationship criticized because the woman loves a man who is married to someone else. How does this differ from the situation in this excerpt from A Midsummer Night's Dream?

a. Hermia and Lysander do not actually love each other.
b. Hermia and Lysander are only involved with each other.
c. Hermia and Demetrious are not yet married.
d. Hermia and Demetrious are being kept apart by her father.

Questions 11-15 pertain to the following excerpt.

The United States Bill of Rights

Article I. After the first enumeration required by the first article of the Constitution, there shall be one representative for every thirty thousand, until the number shall amount to one hundred, after which the proportion shall be so regulated by Congress, that there shall not be less than one hundred representatives, nor less than one representative for every forty thousand persons, until the number of representatives shall amount to two hundred, after which the proportion shall be so regulated by Congress, that there shall not be less than two hundred representatives, nor more than one representative for every fifty thousand.

Article II. No law varying the compensation for services of the senators and representatives shall take effect, until an election of representatives shall have intervened.

Article III. Congress shall make no law respecting an establishment of religion, or prohibiting the free exercise thereof, or abridging the freedom of speech, or of the press, or the right of the people peaceably to assemble, and to petition the government for a redress of grievances.

Article IV. A well-regulated militia being necessary to the security of a free state, the right of the people to keep and bear arms shall not be infringed.

Article V. No soldier shall, in time of peace, be quartered in any house without the consent of the owner, nor in time of war, but in a manner prescribed by law.

Article VI. The right of the people to be secure in their persons, houses, papers, effects, against unreasonable searches and seizures, shall not be violated; and no warrants shall issue, but upon principal cause, supported by oath or affirmation, and particularly describing the place to be searched, and the persons or things to be seized.

Article VII. No person shall be held to answer for a capital or otherwise infamous crime, unless on a presentment or indictment of a grand jury, except in cases arising in the land or naval forces, or in the militia when in actual service, in time of war or public danger; nor shall any person be subject, for the same offence, to be twice put in jeopardy of life or limb; nor shall be compelled, in any criminal case, to be a witness against himself; nor be deprived of life, liberty, or property, without due process of law; nor shall private property be taken for public use without just compensation.

Article VIII. In all criminal prosecutions, the accused shall enjoy the right of a speedy and public trial, by an impartial jury of the state and district wherein the crime shall have been committed, which district shall have been previously ascertained by law; and to be informed of the nature and cause of the accusation; to be confronted with the witnesses against him; to have compulsory process for obtaining witnesses in his favor; and to have the assistance of counsel for his defense.

Article IX. In suits at common law, where the value in controversy shall exceed twenty dollars, the right of trial by jury shall be preserved, and no fact tried by a jury shall be otherwise reexamined, in any court of the United States, than according to the rules in common law.

Article X. Excessive bail shall not be required, nor excessive fines imposed, nor cruel and unusual punishments inflicted.

Article XI. The enumeration, in the Constitution, of certain rights, shall not be construed to deny or disparage others retained by the people.

Article XII. The powers not delegated to the United States by the Constitution, nor prohibited by it to the states, are reserved to the states, respectively, or to the people.

11. What is a purpose of Article III?

a. placing limitations on harmful speech
b. maintaining the separation of church and state
c. listing common grievances against the government
d. encouraging people to assemble peaceably

12. Which Article protects privacy and ownership?

a. Article II
b. Article III
c. Article IV
d. Article V

This question has two parts. Answer Part A, then answer Part B.

13. Part A: What idea recurs in Articles VI through XI?

a. the protection of the property and rights of those accused of committing a crime
b. the protection of the victims and the perpetrators of violent crimes
c. the insurance that criminal trials are conducted efficiently and quickly
d. the insurance that property is not illegally seized or searched

Part B: Which quote from the excerpt best supports your answer in Part A?

a. be quartered in any house without the consent of the owner
b. and no warrants shall issue
c. the accused shall enjoy the right of a speedy and public trial,
d. The powers not delegated to the United States by the Constitution,

14. Which of the following sources would prove best to consult if disputing the contents of the Bill of Rights?

a. someone considered an expert on the document
b. a reprint of the document in a school textbook
c. a photo of the document on the Internet
d. the original documents

15. Why is the Bill of Rights divided into brief sections?

a. to emphasize the fluidness of its prose
b. to draw attention to its most important sections
c. to make it well organized and clear
d. to place the most important sections first

Questions 16-20 pertain to the following excerpt.

Excerpt from President Woodrow Wilson's 1919 Address in Favor of the League of Nations

It gives me pleasure to add to this formal reading of the result of our labors that the character of the discussion, which occurred at the sittings of the commission was not only of the most constructive but of the most encouraging sort. It was obvious throughout our discussions that, although there were subjects upon which there were individual differences of judgment with regard to the method by which our objects should be obtained, there was practically at no point any serious differences of opinion or motive as to the objects which we were seeking.

Indeed, while these debates were not made the opportunity for the expression of enthusiasm and sentiments, I think the other members of the commission will agree with me that there was an undertone of high respect and of enthusiasm for the thing we were trying to do which was heartening throughout everything.

Because we felt that in a way this conference did entrust into us the expression of one of its highest and most important purposes, to see to it that the concord of the world in the future with regard to the objects of justice should not be subject to doubt or uncertainty; that the cooperation of the great body of nations should be assured in the maintenance of peace upon terms of honor and of international obligations.

The compulsion of that task was constantly upon us, and at no point was there shown the slightest desire to do anything but suggest the best means to accomplish that great object. There is very great significance, therefore, in the fact that the result was reached unanimously.

Fourteen nations were represented, among them all of those powers which for convenience we have called the Great Powers, and among the rest a representation of the greatest variety of circumstances and interests. So that I think we are justified in saying that the significance of the result, therefore, has the deepest of all meanings, the union of wills in a common purpose, a union of wills which cannot be resisted and which, I dare say, no nation will run the risk of attempting to resist.

Now, as to the character of the document. While it has consumed some time to read this document, I think you will see at once that it is very simple, and in nothing so simple as in the structure which it suggests for a league of nations, a body of delegates, an executive council, and a permanent secretariat.

When it came to the question of determining the character of the representation in the Body of Delegates, we were all aware of a feeling which is current throughout the world.

Inasmuch as I am stating it in the presence of the official representatives of the various governments here present, including myself, I may say that there is a universal feeling that the world cannot rest satisfied with merely official guidance. There has reached us through many channels the feeling that if the deliberating body of the League of Nations was merely to be a body of officials representing the various governments, the peoples of the world would not be sure that some of the mistakes which preoccupied officials had admittedly made might not be repeated.

It was impossible to conceive a method or an assembly so large and various as to be really representative of the great body of the peoples of the world, because, as I roughly reckon it, we represent as we sit around this table more than 1.2 billion people.

You cannot have a representative assembly of 1.2 billion people, but if you leave it to each government to have, if it pleases, one or two or three representatives, though only with a single vote, it may vary its representation from time to time, not only, but it may (originate) the choice of its several representatives [wireless here unintelligible.

Therefore we thought that this was a proper and a very prudent concession to the practically universal opinion of plain men everywhere that they wanted the door left open to a variety of representation. instead of being confined to a single official body with which they could or might not find themselves in sympathy.

And you will notice that this body has unlimited rights of discussion. I mean of discussion of anything that falls within the field of international relations—and that it is especially agreed that war or international misunderstandings or anything that may lead to friction or trouble is everybody's business, because it may affect the peace of the world.

16. What is the purpose of the first paragraph of the address?

a. to describe the provisions of the League of Nations in extensive detail for those persons not present at its creation
b. to establish an agreeable tone in order to unite those persons with disagreements regarding the League of Nations
c. to explain the difficult and often heated process of mapping out the League of Nations
d. to illustrate why the League of Nations is essential and how it will help resolve international disagreements

17. What effect does Wilson's recurring use of the word we have on his audience?

a. It purposely avoids mentioning any of the creators of the League of Nations by name.
b. It places blame for the League of Nations on both himself and his audience.
c. It emphasizes the creation of the League of Nations as a collective process.
d. It creates the sense that everyone involved in debating the League of Nations agreed with him.

18. Why does Wilson say, "You cannot have a representative assembly of 1.2 billion people"?

a. to illustrate the necessity of government representatives
b. to prove that large groups of people are unruly
c. to marvel at how many people will benefit from the League of Nations
d. to show how the methods of the past have failed

19. What are the "Great Powers"?

a. the League of Nations' abilities to represent people
b. the fourteen nations comprising the League of Nations
c. the 1.2 billion people the League of Nations represents
d. the people who first conceived of the League of Nations

This question has two parts. Answer Part A, then answer Part B.

20. Part A: As used in paragraph one of the excerpt, the word "commission" means

a. task
b. accredit
c. acquisition
d. committee

Part B: Which word from paragraph one gives you the best clue as to the meaning of "commission" in Part A?

a. occurred
b. sittings
c. acquisition
d. constructive

Questions 21 -29 pertain to the following passages:

Alice's Adventures in Wonderland

By Lewis Carroll

(1) Alice was beginning to get very tired of sitting by her sister on the bank, and of having nothing to do: once or twice she had peeped into the book her sister was reading, but it had no pictures or conversations in it, 'and what is the use of a book,' thought Alice 'without pictures or conversation?'

(2) So she was considering in her own mind (as well as she could, for the hot day made her feel very sleepy and stupid), whether the pleasure of making a daisy-chain would be worth the trouble of getting up and picking the daisies, when suddenly a White Rabbit with pink eyes ran close by her.

(3) There was nothing so VERY remarkable in that; nor did Alice think it so VERY much out of the way to hear the Rabbit say to itself, 'Oh dear! Oh dear! I shall be late!' (when she thought it over afterwards, it occurred to her that she ought to have wondered at this, but at the time it all seemed

quite natural); but when the Rabbit actually TOOK A WATCH OUT OF ITS WAISTCOAT-POCKET, and looked at it, and then hurried on, Alice started to her feet, for it flashed across her mind that she had never before seen a rabbit with either a waistcoat-pocket, or a watch to take out of it, and burning with curiosity, she ran across the field after it, and fortunately was just in time to see it pop down a large rabbit-hole under the hedge.

(4) In another moment down went Alice after it, never once considering how in the world she was to get out again.

(5) The rabbit-hole went straight on like a tunnel for some way, and then dipped suddenly down, so suddenly that Alice had not a moment to think about stopping herself before she found herself falling down a very deep well.

(6) Either the well was very deep, or she fell very slowly, for she had plenty of time as she went down to look about her and to wonder what was going to happen next. First, she tried to look down and make out what she was coming to, but it was too dark to see anything; then she looked at the sides of the well, and noticed that they were filled with cupboards and book-shelves; here and there she saw maps and pictures hung upon pegs. She took down a jar from one of the shelves as she passed; it was labelled 'ORANGE MARMALADE', but to her great disappointment it was empty: she did not like to drop the jar for fear of killing somebody, so managed to put it into one of the cupboards as she fell past it.

(7) 'Well!' thought Alice to herself, 'after such a fall as this, I shall think nothing of tumbling down stairs! How brave they'll all think me at home! Why, I wouldn't say anything about it, even if I fell off the top of the house!' (Which was very likely true.)

(8) Down, down, down. Would the fall NEVER come to an end! 'I wonder how many miles I've fallen by this time?' she said aloud. 'I must be getting somewhere near the centre of the earth. Let me see: that would be four thousand miles down, I think—' (for, you see, Alice had learnt several things of this sort in her lessons in the schoolroom, and though this was not a VERY good opportunity for showing off her knowledge, as there was no one to listen to her, still it was good practice to say it over) '—yes, that's about the right distance—but then I wonder what Latitude or Longitude I've got to?' (Alice had no idea what Latitude was, or Longitude either, but thought they were nice grand words to say.)

(9) Presently she began again. 'I wonder if I shall fall right THROUGH the earth! How funny it'll seem to come out among the people that walk with their heads downward! The Antipathies, I think—' (she was rather glad there WAS no one listening, this time, as it didn't sound at all the right word) '—but I shall have to ask them what the name of the country is, you know. Please, Ma'am, is this New Zealand or Australia?' (and she tried to curtsey as she spoke—fancy CURTSEYING as you're falling through the air! Do you think you could manage it?) 'And what an ignorant little girl she'll think me for asking! No, it'll never do to ask: perhaps I shall see it written up somewhere.'

(10) Down, down, down. There was nothing else to do, so Alice soon began talking again. 'Dinah'll miss me very much to-night, I should think!' (Dinah was the cat.) 'I hope they'll remember her saucer of milk at tea-time. Dinah my dear! I wish you were down here with me! There are no mice in the air, I'm afraid, but you might catch a bat, and that's very like a mouse, you know. But do cats eat bats, I wonder?' And here Alice began to get rather sleepy, and went on saying to herself, in a dreamy sort of way, 'Do cats eat bats? Do cats eat bats?' and sometimes, 'Do bats eat cats?' for, you see, as she couldn't answer either question, it didn't much matter which way she put it. She felt that she was dozing off, and had just begun to dream that she was walking hand in hand with Dinah, and

saying to her very earnestly, 'Now, Dinah, tell me the truth: did you ever eat a bat?' when suddenly, thump! thump! down she came upon a heap of sticks and dry leaves, and the fall was over.

(11) Alice was not a bit hurt, and she jumped up on to her feet in a moment: she looked up, but it was all dark overhead; before her was another long passage, and the White Rabbit was still in sight, hurrying down it. There was not a moment to be lost: away went Alice like the wind, and was just in time to hear it say, as it turned a corner, 'Oh my ears and whiskers, how late it's getting!' She was close behind it when she turned the corner, but the Rabbit was no longer to be seen: she found herself in a long, low hall, which was lit up by a row of lamps hanging from the roof.

(12) There were doors all round the hall, but they were all locked; and when Alice had been all the way down one side and up the other, trying every door, she walked sadly down the middle, wondering how she was ever to get out again.

(13) Suddenly she came upon a little three-legged table, all made of solid glass; there was nothing on it except a tiny golden key, and Alice's first thought was that it might belong to one of the doors of the hall; but, alas! either the locks were too large, or the key was too small, but at any rate it would not open any of them. However, on the second time round, she came upon a low curtain she had not noticed before, and behind it was a little door about fifteen inches high: she tried the little golden key in the lock, and to her great delight it fitted!

(14) Alice opened the door and found that it led into a small passage, not much larger than a rat-hole: she knelt down and looked along the passage into the loveliest garden you ever saw. How she longed to get out of that dark hall, and wander about among those beds of bright flowers and those cool fountains, but she could not even get her head through the doorway; 'and even if my head would go through,' thought poor Alice, 'it would be of very little use without my shoulders. Oh, how I wish I could shut up like a telescope! I think I could, if I only know how to begin.' For, you see, so many out-of-the-way things had happened lately, that Alice had begun to think that very few things indeed were really impossible.

(15) There seemed to be no use in waiting by the little door, so she went back to the table, half hoping she might find another key on it, or at any rate a book of rules for shutting people up like telescopes: this time she found a little bottle on it, ('which certainly was not here before,' said Alice,) and round the neck of the bottle was a paper label, with the words 'DRINK ME' beautifully printed on it in large letters.

(16) It was all very well to say 'Drink me,' but the wise little Alice was not going to do THAT in a hurry. 'No, I'll look first,' she said, 'and see whether it's marked "poison" or not'; for she had read several nice little histories about children who had got burnt, and eaten up by wild beasts and other unpleasant things, all because they WOULD not remember the simple rules their friends had taught them: such as, that a red-hot poker will burn you if you hold it too long; and that if you cut your finger VERY deeply with a knife, it usually bleeds; and she had never forgotten that, if you drink much from a bottle marked 'poison,' it is almost certain to disagree with you, sooner or later.

(17) However, this bottle was NOT marked 'poison,' so Alice ventured to taste it, and finding it very nice, (it had, in fact, a sort of mixed flavour of cherry-tart, custard, pine-apple, roast turkey, toffee, and hot buttered toast,) she very soon finished it off.

(18) 'What a curious feeling!' said Alice; 'I must be shutting up like a telescope.'

(19) And so it was indeed: she was now only ten inches high, and her face brightened up at the thought that she was now the right size for going through the little door into that lovely garden.

First, however, she waited for a few minutes to see if she was going to shrink any further: she felt a little nervous about this; 'for it might end, you know,' said Alice to herself, 'in my going out altogether, like a candle. I wonder what I should be like then?' And she tried to fancy what the flame of a candle is like after the candle is blown out, for she could not remember ever having seen such a thing.

21. Read the following dictionary entry:

Burning [bur-ning] adjective (1) intense or urgent (2) very hot (3) on fire, with visible flames (4) a feeling caused by some kind of fire or heat

Which definition best matches the meaning of "burning" as it is used in paragraph 3?

a. Definition 1
b. Definition 2
c. Definition 3
d. Definition 4

22. How does the setting at the beginning of the story contribute to Alice's decision to follow the White Rabbit?

a. It makes her feel sleepy
b. It makes her feel restless
c. It makes her feel curious
d. It makes her feel like reading

23. Why might Alice use the words *latitude* and *longitude* in paragraph 8?

a. She wants to find her exact location on the map.
b. She wants to show off her knowledge of big words.
c. She wants to see if her words echo down the hole.
d. She wants to say big words even if she doesn't know exactly what they mean.

24. Why has the author capitalized the words *through, was,* and *curtseying* in paragraph 9?

a. To mark them as words that need to be proofread
b. To emphasize their meaning
c. To show that Alice is upset by falling
d. To indicate that Alice is talking to someone

25. Alice's decision to drink the liquid in the bottle in paragraphs 15-17 can be described as...

a. Thoughtful
b. Angry
c. Wild
d. Unreasonable

26. Why does Alice feel nervous in paragraph 19?

a. She thinks the liquid might be poison
b. She is afraid that the liquid isn't working
c. She is worried that she will keep shrinking
d. She is nervous that she will turn into a flame

This question has two parts. Answer Part A, then answer Part B.

27. From the description in paragraphs 6-10, the reader can tell that...

a. Alice is in great danger
b. Alice is very nervous
c. The story will be realistic
d. The story will be fantastical

Part B: Which sentence from paragraphs 6-10 best supports your answer in Part A?

a. How brave they'll all think me at home!
b. Presently she began again.
c. 'And what an ignorant little girl she'll think me for asking!
d. 'I wonder if I shall fall right THROUGH the earth!

28. What is Alice's problem in paragraph 14?

a. She can't fit the key into any of the doors
b. She can't fit through the door that the key opens
c. She is shrinking
d. She is in a strange, unknown setting

29. What is the author indicating is most unusual about the rabbit described in paragraphs 2 and 3?

a. It has pink eyes
b. It is speaking
c. It has a watch
d. It jumps down a rabbit hole

Questions 30 – 35 pertain to the following letter:

Letters from an Oklahoman Abroad
By Carrie LeFlore Perry

Montreal

Mother Mine:

(1) Out of the United States! We passed across the lake from Lewiston to Toronto and finding a couple of hours at our disposal, we proceeded to "do" the town. I cannot say it is especially interesting; it is clean and hustling, but too much like an American city to please me. You see, I am looking for the old, the beautiful and the picturesque, not the new and practical. The night was so cool I slept like a child and awoke at five-thirty ready to enjoy the Thousand Islands. I think a picture of an openmouthed rustic and a whole row of exclamation points would give you a better idea of my state this morning than words. Island after island, bearing homes of splendor, then dear little wooded spots with an unpretentious cottage peeping from the trees; again, a monster club house and magnificent grounds, just one continuous picture of homes and places of pleasure. Many of the houses crowning the islands were such monster affairs the lawns were lost in the river! Do they have babies in those homes? If so, how do they keep them out of the water? Ed chuckled with pleasure over the mental picture of you, on a little pocket-handkerchief lawn, with those irrepressible boys, in a wild endeavor to keep them out of the St. Lawrence!

(2) The early morning light added to the magic beauty of the scene, yet I shall be disappointed if the Rhine is not more entrancing.

(3) The castles are too new, the homes do not show the caress of time; it is like our entire country, great and beautiful, but so new, so palpably new. We were from six to ten-thirty passing through this wonderful bit of the St. Lawrence, and like unto children, we were quite sure the island of the moment was the most fair.

(4) We were told that there were 1,642 in all, and I do not doubt the statement after this morning. Leaving Prescott where we changed to a smaller boat, we were soon passing the numerous rapids. They increased in wonder until the Lachine Rapids were entered, and there we were truly amazed! A lady friend had informed me that I would be greatly disappointed with the rapids, as they were very peaceful, like unto soap bubbles! My comment is this: I would not wish that brand of soap turned loose in my vicinity if I were boating. Do you recall the legend of the Indian, who, for telling a lie, was doomed by the Great Spirit to ever wander by streams with his canoe upon his back in a fruitless search for a place to launch it? I wonder if he ever tried the Lachine Rapids? If he did I'll venture the Great Spirit had to hurry to save man and canoe. When we reached Cornwall, we found the bridge had fallen, blocking the canal, and learned our boat would be the last to Montreal for several days. You see the vessels go down the river but up the canal, because of the rapids. I am so thankful we did not miss our river trip.

(5) We are staying at a quaint old hotel, in the French part of the city, very near the cathedral where Ed was christened. You need a guide in the hotel; it is a succession of up you go and down you come! There is an air of age and an odor too, about the rooms and corridors. We were told the present King stayed here, when he visited Canada as Prince of Wales, and I feel sure there has been little change since then! We have a monster apartment lined with mirrors and such massive furniture I feel oppressed. I tried to find the office before commencing this letter, and landed in an unknown hall. Seeing a chambermaid I inquired the way to the elevator. and was told something like this: Up two stairs, around a corner, down three steps, a long corridor, up three, then up two, across a hall, and enter the elevator and I would soon find myself opposite the office! I appreciated her directions but begged her to escort me to room 45 as I would defer the excursion until my husband returned.

(6) I wish I could find my way to the hall of the lion; it is rather exciting to press a button, see the monster tongue loll out, and then a stream of ice water. Would not the boys drink to repletion?

June 24

(7) Mother, Ed came in just as I was finishing the above paragraph, and with his assistance I found the lion and also enjoyed a street car ride. Today we have been "sight-seeing." Right here I wish to say that Ed would be a capital guide, he will even sacrifice truth to interest if he is not sure of his data. You would never suspect it, but I have a lurking suspicion that I have been told many dream tales, although what of it? May not a man romance of his home city? The very first thing we did was to make our way across the historic Place D Armes Square into the old cathedral. It is a place of shadows, where prayer comes easily to the heart; beneath the giant crucifix of our Lord thereon, the soul is melted with tenderness.

(8) I did so wish to examine the records and see his name there, as a tiny infant, but we were too early, and later in the day we would be elsewhere. We had decided to have breakfast in the Café A--, where Ed assured me the delicacies offered were beyond compare, and the room a little palace. Ah, the eyes of childhood! When we entered the small place, Ed with a twinkle said: "My dear, this place has grown smaller; I assure you it used to be the size of the cathedral!" Dear old café, perhaps it had seen better days; I know I have never seen a poorer breakfast. I drank to the King, in a cup of awful liquid called English Breakfast tea. Heaven pity the subjects of King Edward if they drink that decoction frequently! After a most unsatisfactory repast Ed said: "Now we will buy the very finest peppermints in the world; the kind I used to eat." Alas for the dreams of childhood, the candy was the "last straw." When we reached the street it was my turn and I said, "Let us buy presidents at a baker shop, you know dear, the kind you used to buy in old Montreal." You see I was determined to finish the "dream" right then and there. Cruel of me, I hear you say? Do believe me, that pastry was delicious, the very best ever; I shall urge all my friends to visit Montreal and eat "Presidents." We walked on old Bleury Street to the Jesuit College where his young ideas were encourage to burst into bloom, and there I met an old priest who knew Ed as a boy, and had the pleasure (?) of teaching him. He assured me that Ed's ideas were always ready to bloom and ofttimes the flowers were startling.

(9) No one feared he would die early because of his angelic goodness, but they often expected him to enter the pearly gates in a violent manner. He was permitted to lead me through his former class room, recreation room, and out-door play grounds; it was quite interesting to see the places and hear his animated tales of old school days.

(10) From the College to Mount Royal on the cars it is but a little time, and there we were high above the city, enjoying the wondrous panorama. Ed pointed out all the historic houses and thus I have learned my Montreal fairly well, even if here but a day. This is a city of churches and charitable institutions, if we had more time we would surely visit many of them; I am not fully content with a "bird's eye view." When we returned to the hotel, while I rested Ed went out to see a college chum who is now a dignified attorney; he must have had a jolly time as he was quite late returning to the hotel for me, and our little excursion to the Convent of the Ladies of the Sacred Heart was begun as the afternoon was almost ended.

(11) The trolley ride was so cool and through such fine country I was rather sorry when the convent cross appeared. Madame K., my old teacher, gave us welcome and showed us the many beauties of the place. It was such a comfort to talk with dear Madam, I felt that she was truly interested in all that concerned me. After a pleasant hour, we turned our faces towards Montreal; the lamps were glowing when we reached the city and thus our pleasure was enhanced, it lies so quaint and queer under the gleaming lights. After a dinner--not at the Café A.--we strolled along the streets of the French town and Ed aired his mother-tongue with the many children scampering here and there in the joys of hide and seek. Thus ends our day in Montreal; we are true birds of passage, in twenty minutes we leave for Quebec, and until then you will have peace.

Lovingly,

C.

30. In paragraph 8, the word "repast" refers to...

a. English Breakfast tea
b. Breakfast
c. Peppermints
d. King Edward

This question has two parts. Answer Part A, then answer Part B.

31. Part A: Paragraphs 1-3 are mainly about the narrator...

a. Sightseeing across the United States
b. Exploring the castles along the Rhine river
c. Going down the St. Lawrence river to see both mansions and cottages
d. Watching children play in the river

Part B: Which sentence from the letter best supports your answer from Part A?

a. We passed across the lake from Lewiston to Toronto and finding a couple of hours at our disposal, we proceeded to "do" the town.
b. Island after island, bearing homes of splendor, then dear little wooded spots with an unpretentious cottage peeping from the trees; again, a monster club house and magnificent grounds, just one continuous picture of homes and places of pleasure.
c. Out of the United States!
d. If so, how do they keep them out of the water?

32. Why does the narrator find the "Thousand Islands" to be disappointing?

a. She thinks that the homes don't look old enough
b. She is displeased that the cottages and castles are so old
c. She is angry that the name of the islands is the Thousand Islands when there are really 1,642 islands
d. There were too many children around

33. How did the narrator learn about Montreal?

a. By touring the Thousand Islands
b. By eating at Café A
c. By viewing the city from Mount Royal
d. By chatting with Madame K.

34. What is the narrator's purpose in writing this selection?

a. To write a travel book
b. To visit Montreal
c. To remember her childhood
d. To describe her visit to Montreal

35. In paragraph 8, why does the narrator place a question mark after the word "pleasure"?

a. She is unsure if she spelled the word correctly
b. She has not decided if she likes the priest
c. She jokingly thinks that it would have been unpleasant to teach Ed
d. She is not sure if the priest was really Ed's teacher

Use "Alice's Adventures in Wonderland" and "Letters from an Oklahoman" to answer questions 36-38:

36. What is something that Alice from *Alice's Adventures in Wonderland* and the narrator of *Letters from an Oklahoman Abroad* have in common?

a. They are both traveling with companions
b. They are both experiencing something new
c. They are both seeing strange, fantastical things
d. They are both journeying by boat

37. What emotion does the narrator of Letters from an Oklahoman Abroad and Alice from Alice's Adventures in Wonderland share?

a. Curiosity
b. Fear
c. Disappointment
d. Excitement

38. The two passages both contain...

a. Unique animals.
b. Memories.
c. Historic buildings.
d. A journey.

Questions 39-40 pertain to the following visual representation:

Aisha is packing for a trip. See her list below:

39. Based on the list of items, where could the reader infer Aisha might be going?

a. The rainforest
b. The desert
c. The mountains
d. A tropical beach

40. What's the most logical reason why Aisha might be packing more short sleeve shirts than long sleeve ones?

a. She's worried that some of the short sleeve shirts will get lost
b. She thinks it's more likely to be hot than cold
c. She only has five long sleeve shirts
d. She doesn't want to run out of room in her suitcase

Short answer questions

In "Alice's Adventures in Wonderland," what techniques does the author use to illustrate Alice's personality? Use examples from the text to explain your answer.

Answers and Explanations

1. D: With its grotesque carvings, excessive slants, and thorny vegetation, Wuthering Heights is a strange and foreboding house. As such, the author's description contributes to the story's strange and foreboding tone. Although Mr. Lockwood seems to like the house, its description alone does not explain why he likes it. Furthermore, although a misanthrope might live in a foreboding house, this fact alone does not prove Heathcliff's misanthropy.

2. B: Although this excerpt is not overly comedic, the narrator, Mr. Lockwood, makes a few sarcastic remarks. Sarcasm combines harshness and humor. When Lockwood remarks that Joseph is sour that he "must have need of divine aid to digest his dinner," he does not mean that Joseph literally needs God's help to digest. Instead, he is making a sarcastic joke about Joseph's sourness.

3. D: Mr. Lockwood describes the ventilation as bracing. Ventilation allows the flow of cool, fresh air, which can create an invigorating sensation. Although the word bracing can mean, "supporting," "bracketing," and "staying," this is not how the author uses the word in paragraph 8.

4. C: Heathcliff seems to have little regard for his old home. He does not garden and does not have a gardening staff. As a result, the vegetation on his property will be trimmed and landscaped only if his cattle decide to nibble it. Although the statement is somewhat humorous and possibly eccentric, it does not provide evidence that Heathcliff is mad.

5. A: During the 1800s, critics were less inclined to appreciate unlikable characters. The three characters introduced in this excerpt may fit that description for many readers. Heathcliff is described as a misanthrope, or someone who hates people. Joseph is sour, which means he always seems displeased. Mr. Lockwood seems to take great pleasure in the disagreeability of these characters, as well as the house, Wuthering Heights. Critics found these qualities off-putting when Emily Bronte's novel was published in 1847.

6. B: Theseus explicitly asks Hippolyta to come with him, and he tells Demetrius and Egeus that he has "some business against our nuptial" to discuss with them. Although this scene establishes the love between Lysander and Hermia, which likely will be discussed as the scene proceeds, the reader cannot know this for certain from this excerpt.

7. D: In his second block of dialog in the excerpt, Egeus accuses Lysander of doing several things to win his daughter Hermia's love. Egeus says that Lysander "interchanged love-tokens with my child," which means Lysander gave her gifts. He says that Lysander sang to her by moonlight and had "given her rhymes," which refers to poetry. Lysander did paint her portrait.

8. C: Lysander is in love with Hermia and wants to marry her, but she is supposed to marry Demetrius. However, Lysander and Theseus reveal that Demetrius actually loves a woman named Helena. Because they are already romantically involved with the men, Helena clearly knows Demetrius loves her, and Hermia knows Lysander loves her. Although Egeus wants to keep these couples apart for his own selfish reasons, there is no reason to believe the couples are not right for each other.

9. A: Hermia's father, Egeus, is powerful, and he demands that she marry Demetrius. She realizes that her failure to marry Demetrius will bring about negative consequences, and she reveals this knowledge by saying she knows "The worst that may befall me in this case, / If I refuse to wed Demetrius." These lines imply a high cost if she refuses to marry Demetrius and continues to pursue her relationship with Lysander.

10. C: The Scarlett Letter concerns an adulterous relationship. Hermia is not yet married to Demetrious, so her relationship with Lysander is not adulterous. Since Hermia is supposed to marry Demetrious, it is not true that she is only involved with Lysander, even though he is the only man she loves. Hermia's father, Egeus, wants to keep her and Lysander apart, not she and Demetrious, whom he wants her to marry.

11. B: Article III states, "Congress shall make no law respecting an establishment of religion." Not using government to enforce the establishment of a single religion is one way to maintain a separation of church (religion) and state (government). Although the Article defends the right of people to assemble peaceably, it does not encourage such activities outright. The Article refers to grievances against the government but does not list them, nor does it mention anything about harmful speech.

12. D: Article V protects homeowners and the privacy of their homes by stating that soldiers may not be quartered, or live, in their homes without the homeowners consent. Article IV protects the right to own weapons, but it does not make any mention of privacy.

13. Part A: A: Articles VI through XI all deal with protecting the property and rights of those accused of committing a crime. These articles ensure the accused are not subjected to unfair searches or arrests and entitled to a fair trial before a grand jury. The other answer choices do not address everything that Articles VI through XI entail. None of these articles deal with the protection of victims of violent crimes.

Part B: C: This is the only quote from the excerpt that lists a right that someone accused of committing a crime would have. All of the other answers refer to other Articles of the Bill of Rights.

14. D: The best way to validate the information in a document is to consult the original versions, and original copies of it can be viewed in the National Archives and the New York Public Library. Books and people have been known to make mistakes. Photos on the Internet are easily manipulated, so they may not always be reliable.

15. C: James Madison made the Bill of Rights clear and easy to understand by organizing it in short sections devoted to each of its thirteen articles. It is not arranged in order of importance, and its organization does not suggest any articles are more important than others. Fluid prose is not the purpose of this government document.

16. B: Wilson opens his address by acknowledging that some disagreement emerged during the process of creating the League of Nations, but he does not depict these disagreements as heated or angry. Rather, he emphasizes positive words, such as constructive and encouraging. Such terms help establish a peaceful, agreeable tone designed to congratulate and unite persons who had disagreements while creating the League of Nations.

17. C: Wilson's use of the pronoun we united himself and his audience, emphasizing that while he was a leading proponent of the League of Nations, its establishment occurred by way of a collective process. Wilson begins his address by stating that not everyone involved agreed on every issue, which means that some people disagreed with him on certain matters. Nothing in this passage suggests Wilson purposely avoiding mention of any of the League's co-creators by name, nor would he "blame" anyone for helping to create a league of which he was in favor.

18. A: Wilson intended the image of 1.2 billion representatives in a single assembly as somewhat absurd, thereby illustrating the necessity of a much smaller assembly of government representatives. While a group of 1.2 billion people likely would be unruly, this characteristic is not the purpose of Wilson's comment, nor was his purpose to marvel at the great number of people the League of Nations would represent.

19. B: In paragraph four of this excerpt, Wilson says, "Fourteen nations were represented, among them all of those powers which for convenience we have called the Great Powers, and among the rest a representation of the greatest variety of circumstances and interests."

20. Part A: D: In paragraph one, Wilson says, "It gives me pleasure to add to this formal reading of the result of our labors that the character of the discussion, which occurred at the sittings of the commission was not only of the most constructive but of the most encouraging sort." In this context, commission means a group working together to accomplish a goal, in this case, the establishment of the League of Nations. Although commission can be used to mean "task," "accredit," and "acquisition," paragraph one of the excerpt does not use the word any of these ways.

Part B: B: The word "sittings" would give you the best clue as to the meaning of "commission. "Sitting" tells you that a group of people gathered for a meeting, so the only word in Part A that made sense for that was "committee".

21. A: because the passage says that Alice is 'burning with curiosity.' This means that Alice feels an intense curiosity about the White Rabbit. The other three choices are incorrect because they are referring to temperature or fire rather than the intensity of Alice's curiosity.

22. B: because Alice is feeling bored with sitting by her sister and doing nothing, she feels eager to follow the White Rabbit once he appears. Although the first sentence of paragraph 1 says Alice is getting tired, the word 'tired' is not referring to sleepiness, which makes choice A incorrect. Choice C is incorrect because Alice only feels curious after she sees the White Rabbit. The setting, however, makes her feel bored and restless. Choice D is incorrect because Alice says she doesn't feel like reading because her sister's book does not have pictures.

23. D: because Alice says that she has no idea what the words mean but that she thinks they are nice, big words. Choice A is incorrect because, although latitude and longitude can help people find locations on a map, Alice does not know what the words mean. Even though Alice says the words because they're big and impressive, choice B is incorrect because Alice has no one to show off to; she's alone in the rabbit hole. Choice C is incorrect because Alice does not listen for an echo or comment on hearing one.

24. B: is correct because the words are capitalized to emphasize the absurdity of Alice's situation. Choice A is incorrect because this passage is a finished, published excerpt that has already been proofread. Choice C is incorrect because Alice's demeanor shows that she is not upset by falling; in fact, she's intrigued by her new situation. Choice D is incorrect because there is no one else in the rabbit hole that Alice could talk to.

25. A: because Alice examines the bottle and tries to determine if it is poison. Choices B, C, and D are incorrect because Alice is not showing extreme emotion. Instead, she looks at the bottle very analytically and thinks carefully about whether or not she should drink from it.

26. C: the correct answer because Alice is worried that she will continue shrinking and go "out altogether, like a candle." Choice A is incorrect because Alice has already determined that the bottle is not poison. Choice B is incorrect because Alice and the reader have already seen proof that the liquid is working because Alice is getting smaller. Although Alice uses a flame analogy to explain her fears about shrinking forever, choice D is incorrect because Alice is not actually worried about turning into a flame.

27. Part A: D: is the correct answer because details from paragraphs 6-10, such as the extraordinarily long rabbit hole and the cupboards on the walls, show that the story is going to be fantasy. Because it is clear from these details that the story will contain elements that are not real, choice C is incorrect. Although falling through a rabbit hole might seem like a dangerous situation, choice A is incorrect because the passage doesn't convey any sense of urgency or danger. Instead, Alice is experiencing a leisurely fall through the rabbit hole. Choice B is incorrect because Alice portrays curiosity rather than nervousness.

Part B: D: This is the best answer, because it give an example of something that is fantasy. There is no way to fall through the center of the earth.

28. B: because the key only opens a very small door that Alice can't fit through. Choice A is incorrect because the text says that Alice uses the key to open one of the doors. Choice C is incorrect because Alice doesn't start shrinking until paragraph 18, after she drinks the liquid. Choice D is incorrect because Alice has been in a strange, unknown setting for most of the passage, not just in this paragraph.

29. C: Although there are many unusual things about the rabbit, choice C is correct because the author uses capitalization to show the unusualness of the rabbit's watch. Choice A is incorrect because the text says that there is nothing very remarkable in the pink eyes. Choice B is also incorrect because the text says that Alice doesn't think it is that unusual to hear the rabbit speak. Choice D is incorrect because Alice might expect a rabbit to go into a rabbit hole.

30. B: because the narrator says that she and Ed decided to have breakfast at Café A. She also says that she has never seen a worse breakfast. Although she drinks a cup of English Breakfast tea, choice A is not correct because the tea is only one part of the breakfast. Choice C is not correct because they buy the peppermints after they eat the breakfast, or repast. Although the narrator says she pities the subjects of King Edward (the King of England) if they have to drink the awful tea frequently, "repast" isn't referring to the King because it is something that is eaten.

31. Part A: C: because the narrator says that she is taking a boat along the St. Lawrence and comments on the huge castles and small cottages that she sees along the way. Choice A is incorrect because the narrator announces at the beginning of paragraph 1 that she has left the United States. Although the narrator mentions the Rhine River in paragraph 2, she is not on the Rhine yet. She's planning on journeying down the Rhine at a later date and says that she'll be disappointed if it is not more entrancing than the St. Lawrence. Choice D is incorrect because, although the narrator and Ed joke at the image of children playing in the river, they don't actually see any children

Part B: B: This is the best answer because it talks about them going down the river and looking at all of the houses.

32: A: is correct because the narrator comments in paragraph 3 that "the castles are too new, the homes do not show the caress of time…" Choice B is incorrect because she wishes that the cottages and castles were older and is displeased that they are not. Choice C is incorrect because, although the narrator mentions that the Thousand Islands have 1,642 islands, she does not express anger about it. Choice D is incorrect because the narrator does not actually see any children playing while she sails through the Thousand Islands, she only imagines them playing in the river.

33. C: Although the narrator traveled all over Montreal, the best answer is choice C, when she views the city from up high on Mount Royal. She says in paragraph 11 that she is able to learn Montreal fairly well after looking at the city and listening to Ed describe all the buildings. Choice A is incorrect because the narrator sails through the Thousand Islands before arriving in Montreal.

Although the narrator does eat at Café A, which is in Montreal, choice B is incorrect because the café is only one building in the entire city. Choice D is incorrect because Madame K. gives the narrator a tour of Convent of the Ladies of the Sacred Heart, not Montreal.

34. D: because the narrator is describing her visit to Montreal through a letter to her mother. If the narrator wanted to write a travel book, as in choice A, she would have needed to describe the sites she saw in more detail. Instead, she talked more about her experiences. Choice B is incorrect because the narrator's purpose in writing is to describe her visit, which is already in progress. Although the narrator does meet with a teacher from her childhood, choice C is incorrect because the primary purpose is to describe the entire day in Montreal.

35. C: because the narrator is making a joke that it may not have been pleasurable to teach Ed. The reader can determine that it's a joke because the narrator shows affection for Ed throughout the passage. Choice A is incorrect because the narrator does not give any indication that she's worried about the word's spelling. Choice B is incorrect because the narrator does not give her opinion about the priest. Choice D is incorrect because the narrator knows for a fact that the priest taught Ed.

36. B: is the correct answer because both passages are about exploration. In *Letters from an Oklahoman*, the narrator is exploring a new a city, and in *Alice's Adventures in Wonderland*, Alice is discovering a new world. Choice A is incorrect because only the narrator from *Letters* is traveling with a companion (Ed), while Alice is alone in the excerpt. Choice C is incorrect because, although Alice sees a fantastical thing (the talking rabbit with a stopwatch), the narrator from *Letters* doesn't see anything that she believes to be magic. Choice D is incorrect because only the narrator from *Letters* travels by boat; Alice travels by falling down the rabbit hole.

37. A: because both the narrator from *Letters from an Oklahoman* and Alice show curiosity at their new surroundings. The narrator from *Letters* shows curiosity by exploring the different parts of Montreal, and Alice shows curiosity by looking in the cabinets as she falls. While the reader might expect Alice to feel fear as she's falling, she is calm and curious instead, which makes choice B incorrect. The narrator from *Letters* also does not show fear. Choice C is incorrect because only the narrator from *Letters* shows disappointment in the reading excerpts. She has several small moments of disappointment, including after the breakfast at Café A. Choice D is incorrect because only the narrator from *Letters* shows any excitement about her surroundings. The reader might expect Alice to show excitement about her adventure, but she is very calm about her experience.

38. D: because both the narrator from *Letters from an Oklahoman* and Alice are embarking on a journey. Choice A is incorrect because only *Alice's Adventures in Wonderland* contains unique animals. The narrator from *Letters* discusses some of Ed's memories, but choice B is incorrect because Alice doesn't think of any memories. Choice C is incorrect because only the narrator from *Letters* sees historic buildings.

39. C: because all of the items on the list could be used on a mountain. A windbreaker or down jacket could be used when the weather is poor, hiking boots could be used to go for a hike, and shorts could be used in warm weather. Choice A is incorrect because rainforests are not known for cold climates. Choice B is incorrect because it doesn't rain frequently in the desert. Choice D is incorrect because it doesn't typically get cold enough for a down jacket on a tropical beach.

40. B: because it's logical to assume that Aisha is packing the items she thinks she'll need. She may be packing more short-sleeve shirts because she expects to wear them more often. While she may be worried that some of the short sleeve shirts will get lost, choice A is a less logical choice because if Aisha is worried about losing one type of shirt, she's likely worried about both. While it's possible that Aisha only has five long sleeve shirts, choice C is incorrect because it's more logical that Aisha expects to wear the short sleeve shirts more frequently. Choice D is incorrect because there is no indication on the list that Aisha is running out of room in her suitcase.

Short Answer Sample Response

The author does not directly tell the reader about Alice's personality, but he indirectly shows her personality in several places. For example, at the beginning of the passage, the reader learns that Alice gets bored easily and doesn't like sitting around with nothing to do. The author doesn't say this outright, but he shows how Alice doesn't want to sit around with her sister. The author also shows Alice's curiosity by showing her exploring the cabinets in the rabbit hole. He never says that she's curious, but the reader can infer that Alice is a curious person by observing her actions.

How to Overcome Test Anxiety

Just the thought of taking a test is enough to make most people a little nervous. A test is an important event that can have a long-term impact on your future, so it's important to take it seriously and it's natural to feel anxious about performing well. But just because anxiety is normal, that doesn't mean that it's helpful in test taking, or that you should simply accept it as part of your life. Anxiety can have a variety of effects. These effects can be mild, like making you feel slightly nervous, or severe, like blocking your ability to focus or remember even a simple detail.

If you experience test anxiety—whether severe or mild—it's important to know how to beat it. To discover this, first you need to understand what causes test anxiety.

Causes of Test Anxiety

While we often think of anxiety as an uncontrollable emotional state, it can actually be caused by simple, practical things. One of the most common causes of test anxiety is that a person does not feel adequately prepared for their test. This feeling can be the result of many different issues such as poor study habits or lack of organization, but the most common culprit is time management. Starting to study too late, failing to organize your study time to cover all of the material, or being distracted while you study will mean that you're not well prepared for the test. This may lead to cramming the night before, which will cause you to be physically and mentally exhausted for the test. Poor time management also contributes to feelings of stress, fear, and hopelessness as you realize you are not well prepared but don't know what to do about it.

Other times, test anxiety is not related to your preparation for the test but comes from unresolved fear. This may be a past failure on a test, or poor performance on tests in general. It may come from comparing yourself to others who seem to be performing better or from the stress of living up to expectations. Anxiety may be driven by fears of the future—how failure on this test would affect your educational and career goals. These fears are often completely irrational, but they can still negatively impact your test performance.

Elements of Test Anxiety

As mentioned earlier, test anxiety is considered to be an emotional state, but it has physical and mental components as well. Sometimes you may not even realize that you are suffering from test anxiety until you notice the physical symptoms. These can include trembling hands, rapid heartbeat, sweating, nausea, and tense muscles. Extreme anxiety may lead to fainting or vomiting. Obviously, any of these symptoms can have a negative impact on testing. It is important to recognize them as soon as they begin to occur so that you can address the problem before it damages your performance.

The mental components of test anxiety include trouble focusing and inability to remember learned information. During a test, your mind is on high alert, which can help you recall information and stay focused for an extended period of time. However, anxiety interferes with your mind's natural processes, causing you to blank out, even on the questions you know well. The strain of testing during anxiety makes it difficult to stay focused, especially on a test that may take several hours. Extreme anxiety can take a huge mental toll, making it difficult not only to recall test information but even to understand the test questions or pull your thoughts together.

Effects of Test Anxiety

Test anxiety is like a disease—if left untreated, it will get progressively worse. Anxiety leads to poor performance, and this reinforces the feelings of fear and failure, which in turn lead to poor performances on subsequent tests. It can grow from a mild nervousness to a crippling condition. If allowed to progress, test anxiety can have a big impact on your schooling, and consequently on your future.

Test anxiety can spread to other parts of your life. Anxiety on tests can become anxiety in any stressful situation, and blanking on a test can turn into panicking in a job situation. But fortunately, you don't have to let anxiety rule your testing and determine your grades. There are a number of relatively simple steps you can take to move past anxiety and function normally on a test and in the rest of life.

Physical Steps for Beating Test Anxiety

While test anxiety is a serious problem, the good news is that it can be overcome. It doesn't have to control your ability to think and remember information. While it may take time, you can begin taking steps today to beat anxiety.

Just as your first hint that you may be struggling with anxiety comes from the physical symptoms, the first step to treating it is also physical. Rest is crucial for having a clear, strong mind. If you are tired, it is much easier to give in to anxiety. But if you establish good sleep habits, your body and mind will be ready to perform optimally, without the strain of exhaustion. Additionally, sleeping well helps you to retain information better, so you're more likely to recall the answers when you see the test questions.

Getting good sleep means more than going to bed on time. It's important to allow your brain time to relax. Take study breaks from time to time so it doesn't get overworked, and don't study right before bed. Take time to rest your mind before trying to rest your body, or you may find it difficult to fall asleep.

Along with sleep, other aspects of physical health are important in preparing for a test. Good nutrition is vital for good brain function. Sugary foods and drinks may give a burst of energy but this burst is followed by a crash, both physically and emotionally. Instead, fuel your body with protein and vitamin-rich foods.

Also, drink plenty of water. Dehydration can lead to headaches and exhaustion, especially if your brain is already under stress from the rigors of the test. Particularly if your test is a long one, drink water during the breaks. And if possible, take an energy-boosting snack to eat between sections.

Along with sleep and diet, a third important part of physical health is exercise. Maintaining a steady workout schedule is helpful, but even taking 5-minute study breaks to walk can help get your blood pumping faster and clear your head. Exercise also releases endorphins, which contribute to a positive feeling and can help combat test anxiety.

When you nurture your physical health, you are also contributing to your mental health. If your body is healthy, your mind is much more likely to be healthy as well. So take time to rest, nourish your body with healthy food and water, and get moving as much as possible. Taking these physical steps will make you stronger and more able to take the mental steps necessary to overcome test anxiety.

Mental Steps for Beating Test Anxiety

Working on the mental side of test anxiety can be more challenging, but as with the physical side, there are clear steps you can take to overcome it. As mentioned earlier, test anxiety often stems from lack of preparation, so the obvious solution is to prepare for the test. Effective studying may be the most important weapon you have for beating test anxiety, but you can and should employ several other mental tools to combat fear.

First, boost your confidence by reminding yourself of past success—tests or projects that you aced. If you're putting as much effort into preparing for this test as you did for those, there's no reason you should expect to fail here. Work hard to prepare; then trust your preparation.

Second, surround yourself with encouraging people. It can be helpful to find a study group, but be sure that the people you're around will encourage a positive attitude. If you spend time with others who are anxious or cynical, this will only contribute to your own anxiety. Look for others who are motivated to study hard from a desire to succeed, not from a fear of failure.

Third, reward yourself. A test is physically and mentally tiring, even without anxiety, and it can be helpful to have something to look forward to. Plan an activity following the test, regardless of the outcome, such as going to a movie or getting ice cream.

When you are taking the test, if you find yourself beginning to feel anxious, remind yourself that you know the material. Visualize successfully completing the test. Then take a few deep, relaxing breaths and return to it. Work through the questions carefully but with confidence, knowing that you are capable of succeeding.

Developing a healthy mental approach to test taking will also aid in other areas of life. Test anxiety affects more than just the actual test—it can be damaging to your mental health and even contribute to depression. It's important to beat test anxiety before it becomes a problem for more than testing.

Study Strategy

Being prepared for the test is necessary to combat anxiety, but what does being prepared look like? You may study for hours on end and still not feel prepared. What you need is a strategy for test prep. The next few pages outline our recommended steps to help you plan out and conquer the challenge of preparation.

Step 1: Scope Out the Test

Learn everything you can about the format (multiple choice, essay, etc.) and what will be on the test. Gather any study materials, course outlines, or sample exams that may be available. Not only will this help you to prepare, but knowing what to expect can help to alleviate test anxiety.

Step 2: Map Out the Material

Look through the textbook or study guide and make note of how many chapters or sections it has. Then divide these over the time you have. For example, if a book has 15 chapters and you have five days to study, you need to cover three chapters each day. Even better, if you have the time, leave an extra day at the end for overall review after you have gone through the material in depth.

If time is limited, you may need to prioritize the material. Look through it and make note of which sections you think you already have a good grasp on, and which need review. While you are studying, skim quickly through the familiar sections and take more time on the challenging parts.

Write out your plan so you don't get lost as you go. Having a written plan also helps you feel more in control of the study, so anxiety is less likely to arise from feeling overwhelmed at the amount to cover.

Step 3: Gather Your Tools

Decide what study method works best for you. Do you prefer to highlight in the book as you study and then go back over the highlighted portions? Or do you type out notes of the important information? Or is it helpful to make flashcards that you can carry with you? Assemble the pens, index cards, highlighters, post-it notes, and any other materials you may need so you won't be distracted by getting up to find things while you study.

If you're having a hard time retaining the information or organizing your notes, experiment with different methods. For example, try color-coding by subject with colored pens, highlighters, or post-it notes. If you learn better by hearing, try recording yourself reading your notes so you can listen while in the car, working out, or simply sitting at your desk. Ask a friend to quiz you from your flashcards, or try teaching someone the material to solidify it in your mind.

Step 4: Create Your Environment

It's important to avoid distractions while you study. This includes both the obvious distractions like visitors and the subtle distractions like an uncomfortable chair (or a too-comfortable couch that makes you want to fall asleep). Set up the best study environment possible: good lighting and a comfortable work area. If background music helps you focus, you may want to turn it on, but otherwise keep the room quiet. If you are using a computer to take notes, be sure you don't have any other windows open, especially applications like social media, games, or anything else that could distract you. Silence your phone and turn off notifications. Be sure to keep water close by so you stay hydrated while you study (but avoid unhealthy drinks and snacks).

Also, take into account the best time of day to study. Are you freshest first thing in the morning? Try to set aside some time then to work through the material. Is your mind clearer in the afternoon or evening? Schedule your study session then. Another method is to study at the same time of day that you will take the test, so that your brain gets used to working on the material at that time and will be ready to focus at test time.

Step 5: Study!

Once you have done all the study preparation, it's time to settle into the actual studying. Sit down, take a few moments to settle your mind so you can focus, and begin to follow your study plan. Don't give in to distractions or let yourself procrastinate. This is your time to prepare so you'll be ready to fearlessly approach the test. Make the most of the time and stay focused.

Of course, you don't want to burn out. If you study too long you may find that you're not retaining the information very well. Take regular study breaks. For example, taking five minutes out of every hour to walk briskly, breathing deeply and swinging your arms, can help your mind stay fresh.

As you get to the end of each chapter or section, it's a good idea to do a quick review. Remind yourself of what you learned and work on any difficult parts. When you feel that you've mastered the material, move on to the next part. At the end of your study session, briefly skim through your notes again.

But while review is helpful, cramming last minute is NOT. If at all possible, work ahead so that you won't need to fit all your study into the last day. Cramming overloads your brain with more information than it can process and retain, and your tired mind may struggle to recall even previously learned information when it is overwhelmed with last-minute study. Also, the urgent nature of cramming and the stress placed on your brain contribute to anxiety. You'll be more likely to go to the test feeling unprepared and having trouble thinking clearly.

So don't cram, and don't stay up late before the test, even just to review your notes at a leisurely pace. Your brain needs rest more than it needs to go over the information again. In fact, plan to finish your studies by noon or early afternoon the day before the test. Give your brain the rest of the day to relax or focus on other things, and get a good night's sleep. Then you will be fresh for the test and better able to recall what you've studied.

Step 6: Take a Practice Test

Many courses offer sample tests, either online or in the study materials. This is an excellent resource to check whether you have mastered the material, as well as to prepare for the test format and environment.

Check the test format ahead of time: the number of questions, the type (multiple choice, free response, etc.), and the time limit. Then create a plan for working through them. For example, if you have 30 minutes to take a 60-question test, your limit is 30 seconds per question. Spend less time on the questions you know well so that you can take more time on the difficult ones.

If you have time to take several practice tests, take the first one open book, with no time limit. Work through the questions at your own pace and make sure you fully understand them. Gradually work up to taking a test under test conditions: sit at a desk with all study materials put away and set a timer. Pace yourself to make sure you finish the test with time to spare and go back to check your answers if you have time.

After each test, check your answers. On the questions you missed, be sure you understand why you missed them. Did you misread the question (tests can use tricky wording)? Did you forget the information? Or was it something you hadn't learned? Go back and study any shaky areas that the practice tests reveal.

Taking these tests not only helps with your grade, but also aids in combating test anxiety. If you're already used to the test conditions, you're less likely to worry about it, and working through tests until you're scoring well gives you a confidence boost. Go through the practice tests until you feel comfortable, and then you can go into the test knowing that you're ready for it.

Test Tips

On test day, you should be confident, knowing that you've prepared well and are ready to answer the questions. But aside from preparation, there are several test day strategies you can employ to maximize your performance.

First, as stated before, get a good night's sleep the night before the test (and for several nights before that, if possible). Go into the test with a fresh, alert mind rather than staying up late to study.

Try not to change too much about your normal routine on the day of the test. It's important to eat a nutritious breakfast, but if you normally don't eat breakfast at all, consider eating just a protein bar. If you're a coffee drinker, go ahead and have your normal coffee. Just make sure you time it so that the caffeine doesn't wear off right in the middle of your test. Avoid sugary beverages, and drink enough water to stay hydrated but not so much that you need a restroom break 10 minutes into the test. If your test isn't first thing in the morning, consider going for a walk or doing a light workout before the test to get your blood flowing.

Allow yourself enough time to get ready, and leave for the test with plenty of time to spare so you won't have the anxiety of scrambling to arrive in time. Another reason to be early is to select a good seat. It's helpful to sit away from doors and windows, which can be distracting. Find a good seat, get out your supplies, and settle your mind before the test begins.

When the test begins, start by going over the instructions carefully, even if you already know what to expect. Make sure you avoid any careless mistakes by following the directions.

Then begin working through the questions, pacing yourself as you've practiced. If you're not sure on an answer, don't spend too much time on it, and don't let it shake your confidence. Either skip it and come back later, or eliminate as many wrong answers as possible and guess among the remaining ones. Don't dwell on these questions as you continue—put them out of your mind and focus on what lies ahead.

Be sure to read all of the answer choices, even if you're sure the first one is the right answer. Sometimes you'll find a better one if you keep reading. But don't second-guess yourself if you do immediately know the answer. Your gut instinct is usually right. Don't let test anxiety rob you of the information you know.

If you have time at the end of the test (and if the test format allows), go back and review your answers. Be cautious about changing any, since your first instinct tends to be correct, but make sure you didn't misread any of the questions or accidentally mark the wrong answer choice. Look over any you skipped and make an educated guess.

At the end, leave the test feeling confident. You've done your best, so don't waste time worrying about your performance or wishing you could change anything. Instead, celebrate the successful completion of this test. And finally, use this test to learn how to deal with anxiety even better next time.

Review Video: Test Anxiety
Visit mometrix.com/academy and enter code: 100340

Important Qualification

Not all anxiety is created equal. If your test anxiety is causing major issues in your life beyond the classroom or testing center, or if you are experiencing troubling physical symptoms related to your anxiety, it may be a sign of a serious physiological or psychological condition. If this sounds like your situation, we strongly encourage you to seek professional help.

Thank You

We at Mometrix would like to extend our heartfelt thanks to you, our friend and patron, for allowing us to play a part in your journey. It is a privilege to serve people from all walks of life who are unified in their commitment to building the best future they can for themselves.

The preparation you devote to these important testing milestones may be the most valuable educational opportunity you have for making a real difference in your life. We encourage you to put your heart into it—that feeling of succeeding, overcoming, and yes, conquering will be well worth the hours you've invested.

We want to hear your story, your struggles and your successes, and if you see any opportunities for us to improve our materials so we can help others even more effectively in the future, please share that with us as well. **The team at Mometrix would be absolutely thrilled to hear from you!** So please, send us an email (support@mometrix.com) and let's stay in touch.

If you'd like some additional help, check out these other resources we offer for your exam:
http://MometrixFlashcards.com/CCSS

Online Resources

Due to our efforts to try to keep this book to a manageable length, we've created a link that will give you access to all of your online resources:

mometrix.com/resources719/ccg11ela

It's Your Moment, Let's Celebrate It!

Share your story @mometrixtestpreparation